Healing Ableism

Healing Ableism

~

Stories About Disability and Religious Life

DARLA SCHUMM

R

Rutgers University Press

New Brunswick, Camden, and Newark, New Jersey; London and Oxford

Rutgers University Press is a department of Rutgers, The State University
of New Jersey, one of the leading public research universities in the nation.
By publishing worldwide, it furthers the University's mission of dedication
to excellence in teaching, scholarship, research, and clinical care.

Library of Congress Cataloging-in-Publication Data

Names: Schumm, Darla Y. (Darla Yvonne), author
Title: Healing ableism : stories about disability and religious life / Darla Schumm.
Description: New Brunswick, New Jersey : Rutgers University Press, [2025] |
Includes bibliographical references. | Identifiers: LCCN 2025005259 (print) |
LCCN 2025005260 (ebook) | ISBN 9781978842205 paperback |
ISBN 9781978842212 hardcover | ISBN 9781978842229 epub | ISBN 9781978842236 pdf
Subjects: LCSH: People with disabilities—Religious life |
Disabilities—Religious aspects
Classification: LCC BV4910 .S38 2025 (print) | LCC BV4910 (ebook) |
DDC 261.8/324—dc23/eng/20250807
LC record available at https://lccn.loc.gov/2025005259
LC ebook record available at https://lccn.loc.gov/2025005260

A British Cataloging-in-Publication record for this
book is available from the British Library.

References to internet websites (URLs) were accurate at the time of writing.
Neither the author nor Rutgers University Press is responsible for URLs
that may have expired or changed since the manuscript was prepared.

♾ The paper used in this publication meets the requirements of the
American National Standard for Information Sciences—Permanence
of Paper for Printed Library Materials, ANSI Z39.48-1992.

rutgersuniversitypress.org

For Henry, I love you to the moon and back, infinity times

Contents

Healing Ableism

~ 1 ~

Introduction

When I was eight years old, I received a life-changing diagnosis that instantly turned me into a person with a disability. I distinctly remember sitting in Dr. Fall's office at the University of Michigan medical center as he delivered the results of a year of endless eye exams. My parents and I spent the better part of that year traveling to and from our home three hours away in northwestern Indiana for a barrage of tests, trying to figure out why I kept losing vision. Although I did not realize it at the time, the previous year had put my parents on a roller coaster of potential diagnoses and emotional turbulence. One test suggested that I might have a terminal brain tumor; another test indicated that I had an eye condition that would result in total blindness; many other tests were inconclusive, offering no clear answers as to why an eight-year-old girl could no longer read the chalkboard in school from her desk in the front row.

As good and faithful Mennonites—a small Christian Protestant Anabaptist denomination—my parents not only entrusted my care to the rational, secular medical world but also invoked their belief in a benevolent omnipotent God. They invested their hopes in the idea that prayer would play no small part in my eventual diagnosis. I clearly remember an evening sitting among a circle of my parents' church friends after returning home from a day of medical testing. They laid hands on me and fervently prayed for my healing.

Soon after the prayer warriors' intervention, as I like to call it now, our family traveled back to Dr. Fall's office to learn my fate. I cannot imagine how my parents would have felt driving those three hours. Did they believe that the doctors would be able to offer a cure? Did they believe that God would heal me? I do not remember much about what Dr. Fall told me and my parents that day, but he finally had an answer. He named my condition, he described what was happening to my retina and optic nerve from a medical perspective, and he explained what this would mean for my vision. The good news was that I did not have a brain tumor, and my particular diagnosis did not portend total blindness. The less good news was that I was already legally blind, and there was no cure for my disease. Given the other options, however, this really did sound like less good news as opposed to straight up bad news. What I do remember as clearly as what I ate for breakfast just a few hours ago are the words Dr. Fall spoke directly to me. "Young lady," Dr. Fall said in a grandfatherly tone, "there is absolutely nothing you will not be able to do in your life other than drive a car." We traveled home that day full of relief and hope and gratitude. It was not entirely clear to me why this was such a happy outcome, but I was swept up by the palpable elation of my parents and the enthusiastic responses of the prayer warriors whose houses we stopped at to report the good news before returning home.

My eight-year-old self had no idea that that fateful diagnosis had already begun to weave together some of the most fundamental threads of the tapestry of my future personal and professional life. As my familiarity with the prayer circle already suggests, my life up to that point had been immersed in religious practice and community. I grew up in a Mennonite home, my father is a retired Mennonite minister, I attended a Mennonite high school and college, I earned a PhD in religion and teach religious studies, and I am married to an Episcopal priest. While it has taken over forty years to absorb and accept, from that moment on in Dr. Fall's office, I was also a person with a disability. Religion and disability are as intrinsic to my life as breathing. Writing this book, therefore, feels in many respects like one of the most inevitable journeys of my life. But the road from Dr. Fall's office to writing this book was full of many unexpected and delightful—and some not-so-delightful—twists and turns.

The most honest thing I can say about my relationship with both religion and disability is that it's complicated. My religious path appears straightforward enough on the surface: I grew up Mennonite; I flirted with the Quakers for a short time; and in my mid-thirties, I joined the Episcopal Church. Bubbling beneath the surface, however, simmers a lifetime of questions and pushback against almost every religious truth and doctrine I encountered. As a child in either Sunday school or summer Bible school (I can't remember which one), I insisted that the business about three persons in one, or the Trinity, was ridiculous. Midway through high school, I doggedly questioned how Jesus could be simultaneously human and divine. By college, I outright dismissed the presumption that Christianity presented the one "true" way to God. Abandoning church attendance altogether, I spent most Sunday mornings in college at the Olympia Candy Kitchen—a quaint café—with friends discussing things as mundane as what we did the night before and as profound as how to change the world. My postcollege plan was to go immediately to a PhD program in clinical psychology, but after submitting psychology graduate school applications, a friend asked if I had ever considered studying religion instead. I had not. Yet the question lingered. Two years later I matriculated in a master's program in religion and social ethics at the Pacific School of Religion in Berkeley, California.

During college, I had convinced myself that I was finished with religion, but my time in Berkeley reignited a fire for engaging religious questions. I did not return to faith in a confessional sense, but I realized that religious questions were embedded deep in my psyche and soul. Like a magnet, religion pulled me back to an intense intellectual engagement with its central questions. Two years after receiving my MA, I matriculated in a PhD program in religion, ethics, and society at Vanderbilt University in Nashville, Tennessee. If I was surprised to be pursuing a doctoral degree in religion, I was even more surprised to be doing it in the Bible Belt. While at Vanderbilt, I met, fell in love with, and married a man who eventually became an Episcopal priest.

My students often ask what I believe about God. The answer is simple: I believe that there are many paths to divine presence, and no one path is truer than another. I draw on the wisdom of the Dalai Lama, which he imparted at a lecture I attended at the University of Minnesota. He cheerfully encouraged people to wholeheartedly follow their own spiritual path: "If you are Christian, be the best Christian you can be. If you are Buddhist or Hindu, be the best Buddhist or Hindu you can be." A spiritual path is deeply personal and usually determined, at least in part, by external factors such as familial and cultural contexts. Christianity is the tradition with which I am most familiar because it is the religion of my childhood and because when I participate in religious practice these days, it is in an Episcopal church. I do not, however, identify as a Christian in the traditional sense, because that label does not fully encompass the breadth of my beliefs or the nuances of my spirituality.

I identify that day in Dr. Fall's office as the moment when I acquired the label of a person with a disability, but it was many years later before I owned the label, let alone celebrated it. I expended extreme amounts of energy well into adulthood "passing" as a nondisabled person. Through high school I could still read printed books, but only large-print texts. I nonetheless pretended to read regular-size print when I was in public. Even as my vision declined to the point that my process for crossing busy streets involved listening for oncoming cars, saying a quick prayer for safety, hoping that I indeed did not hear any oncoming cars, and then running as fast as I could across the road, I refused to consider mobility aids. I finally agreed to try using a white cane and guide dog after my fiancé broke down in convulsive sobs during a premarital counseling session because he was so worried for my safety every time I left the house alone. Even to this day, when I am without my guide dog, my disability is not necessarily apparent. I still get a mischievous buzz out of "passing" and observing how people squirm when they discover that they unwittingly have been conversing with a blind person.

As a young graduate student, it never occurred to me that disability was a topic for academic consideration. But toward the end of graduate school, I happened upon the late Nancy Eiesland's groundbreaking book, *The Disabled God: Toward a Liberatory Theology of Disability* (1994). Eiesland's text introduced me to disability as a category not only for serious theological reflection but also for rigorous theoretical exploration. Eiesland's work cracked open a new world of intense intellectual and personal engagement with disability.

From my initial encounter with Eiesland's book, my scholarly trajectory took a slow but steady turn toward the emerging field of religion and disability. At the same time, I started shedding the insidious cultural narrative that I had so successfully internalized of disability as tragedy, and I began celebrating disability as one form of human variation, no more or less tragic than other forms of human variety. It is impossible for me to untangle the threads of my deepening acceptance of my disability from the strands of my growing scholarly engagement with the academic field of religion and disability studies, but somewhere along the way, I realized that celebrating my own disability also enriched and informed the texture of my scholarship. These days, my scholarly efforts reside primarily at the nexus of religious studies and disability studies. Always lurking just beneath the surface of my research and writing is the comfortable and often celebrated reality that I am a person with a disability.

The flip side of more fully embracing and celebrating my disability is that I have also increasingly become aware of the ubiquity of ableism. Ableism is an interlocking constellation of parts that are mutually dependent on one another. At its most basic level, ableism is discrimination against people with disabilities. Ableism also entails the assumption that able bodies—that is to say, bodies that function in ways that conform to social and cultural expectations of what is deemed "normal"—are the presumed standard for which social, cultural, and built environments are constructed. Acts of discrimination and entrenched attitudes about embodiment are essential parts of the definition of ableism, but what is most critical to understand about ableism is that, like other oppressive -isms such as sexism, racism, heterosexism, classism, and so on, ableism is embedded in larger systems and structures of domination, power, and privilege. To fully understand ableism, then, is to be aware of the symbiotic relationship between its constitutive parts: literal acts of discrimination; attitudes and beliefs about "normal" embodiment; and how power and privilege simultaneously produce, perpetuate, and reinforce discriminatory acts, attitudes, and beliefs.

Once I started noticing ableism, I found it everywhere. The more I noticed ableism, the more I noticed how infrequently other people notice ableism and how frequently other people are ableist. Unless you have a disability, are a caretaker for someone with a disability, or are the rare person who actually pays attention to forms of discrimination that do not directly affect you or someone you love, you are likely blissfully unaware of the pervasiveness of ableism. And here, dear reader, is the even worse news: I suspect that you, probably without realizing it, say and do stupid, obnoxious, and offensive ableist things. In other words, you unwittingly perpetuate ableism.

Before you launch into your mea culpas for all the times you accidentally said or did something ableist, let me hasten to add that until I began reading disability memoirs, disability theories, activist strategies, and so on, I, too, was kind of an ableist jerk. Scholars call this phenomenon internalized oppression. The term refers to when members of an oppressed group believe, accept, adopt, and perpetuate the negative narratives and beliefs of the oppressor as the unquestioned truth. Gail Pheterson, a feminist writer and psychotherapist, describes internalized oppression as "the incorporation and acceptance by individuals within an oppressed group of the prejudices against them within the dominant society."[1] We can find examples of internalized oppression in many arenas. Take, for example, the long line of women, from U.S. attorney Phyllis Schlafly (1924–2016) to the contemporary Justice Amy Coney Barrett, who actively promote policies, laws, and structures that routinize the subordination of women to men. Or figures like Supreme Court Justice Clarence Thomas (one of two African American Supreme Court justices), who supported the June 2023 majority that gutted affirmative action in college and university admissions decisions. Less public or dramatic examples abound of people with minoritized identities who in their day-to-day lives experience internalized oppression and participate in demeaning themselves and members of the oppressed group to which they belong.

As much as it pains me to admit it, for years I was an expert at internalized oppression. I silently felt superior to other people with disabilities who I did not perceive to be as "productive," smart, or socially smooth as I thought I was. I prided myself on "passing" as a nondisabled person. As I already mentioned, I sometimes went as far as to pretend to read when in public. At least once, the joke was on me because my friend Eric gently pointed out that I was holding the newspaper I was pretending to read upside down! As a graduate student and newly minted PhD, I actively avoided the Religion and Disability Studies Unit at the American Academy of Religion (AAR) conference because, as I told my friend Sally, I did not want able-bodied scholars to dismiss me as a disabled person who only cared about disability scholarship. These days, I swell with pride anytime I am associated with the religion and disability scholars at the AAR because they are among the most cutting-edge, justice-oriented, and intellectually interesting members of the AAR.

If I am being really honest, I had generally avoided other people with disabilities because I had internalized disability "disgust." I carried a heavy load of shame, embarrassment, and anger about my disability. It was easier to ignore my disability when I was surrounded by nondisabled folks who had no real interest in disability because it had no relevance to their privileged, able-bodied lives.

I also embraced the twin of internalized oppression: a belief in minority exceptionalism. This is another way of saying that I thought I was "better" than most people with disabilities and that I thought that being disabled was something to ignore, deny, or hide. The disability community refers to this type of exceptionalism as the "supercrip," a concept I unpack more fully in a later chapter. For now, suffice it to say that a supercrip is someone who does "amazing" things despite their disability. Or someone who does the same things that people without disabilities do, but because they do them with a disability, nondisabled people think it is remarkable that a person with a disability can do unremarkable things. For years, I considered myself a rare supercrip exception and avoided all people and things disability related.

I am not proud of the ways I expressed internalized oppression and minority exceptionalism or how I promoted ableism. I deeply regret how long it took me to accept, embrace, and celebrate my disability and to shed my obnoxious supercrip skin. But here is the thing about internalized oppression: Because we live in a society where ableism oozes in and through every institution, system, organization, structure, ideology, policy, law, and so on, those of us with disabilities will inevitably experience internalized oppression unless we consciously and completely work against ableism.

The process of coming to terms with my disability happened slowly over a period of years. In some ways, it happened without my even knowing that it was happening. There was never a "eureka" moment where I thought, "At last, I am at peace with my disability!" Rather, at some point, I think somewhere in my thirties, I no longer felt angry or sad about being disabled. In fact, I realized that I would not know who I was without it. Disability is a part of who I am, how I understand myself and the world, and most importantly, how I value the perspective that life with a disability affords me. I am often asked if I want to be cured. The honest answer is that I don't know. Yes, my life would be easier in practical ways if I had twenty-twenty vision. But I never wake up in the morning wishing for a cure. I waste no time wishing for a cure.

Although I no longer feel angry about having a disability, I do feel angry about ableism. In fact, I find ableism enraging. I noted earlier that working consciously and completely against ableism is an antidote to internalized oppression. I also maintain that it is important to acknowledge that anger and rage are necessary components of working against ableism. In the context of advancing justice, anger provides valuable information about what is out of balance or wrong with the world. I feel angry about ableism because it limits and denies my full humanity and the full humanity of other disabled people. Rage is an appropriate reaction to the denial of any individual's full humanity.

Yet anger and rage are only useful reactions when they motivate us to restore balance and work toward justice. The late Christian feminist ethicist Beverly Wildung Harrison captures what I am getting at here in the title of one of her best-known essays, "The Power of Anger in the Work of Love."[2] Harrison links anger and love together as constituent parts of justice work. In a similar vein, the Buddhist teacher and activist Lama Rod Owens suggests that anger can be full of wisdom, and when we couple wisdom with compassion, anger transforms into something productive.[3] From this perspective, harnessing the power of anger to work for love and justice is compassionate, hopeful, and sacred work.

Throughout the book, I talk about raging against ableism. For me, the power of raging against ableism is the work of love because it is the work of justice. I am neither an angry nor a rage-filled person. But I embrace rage as one component of the work of love that transforms injustice into justice. In the concluding chapter of the book, I propose accessible love as one vehicle for religious communities that are eager to join me in raging against ableism, but more about that later.

As I began to rage against ableism, I also began wondering about the origins of my internalized oppression and ableist perspectives. How could I effectively rage against ableism if I did not understand its genesis in my own life and worldview? Its origins are in some ways obvious: I did not grow up celebrating disability. I did not grow up thinking that disability was a neutral or regular part of being human. I grew up believing that disability was a tragedy, a lack, something to eliminate if at all possible. The confusing thing about these messages is that while I internalized disability as tragedy, I don't remember specific conversations about disability or disabled people with my family. In fact, I always felt that my family believed that there was nothing wrong with me. My nuclear family treated my disability as just one regular aspect of my identity; they treated me as if I could do anything. Reflecting on my childhood and adolescence now, it is probably most accurate to say that my family thought of me as a supercrip, even though they did not articulate it in those terms. So where did all my internalized oppression and negative messages about disability originate? Put another way, where did I most directly encounter ableism?

Because ableism penetrates all aspects of society, it is impossible to answer these questions definitively. But once I opened Pandora's box, I could not stop exploring the roots of ableism both in my own thinking and in society more generally. I started informally asking other people with disabilities about their experiences of ableism, and before I knew it, I was conducting formal interviews with people with disabilities for a book project (more about this later). One theme kept popping up in these conversations and in my own reflections. Whether because of my context growing up in a relatively insular religious community or because I studied religion and was surrounded by people who paid attention to religion and religious communities, experiences with religious communities, texts, leaders, ideologies, and so on emerged over and over again as a powerful locus of ableism.

I should not have found this surprising. Religion, after all, is one of the most powerful and prevalent shapers of culture and society. I often challenge my students to name a culture that does not include some form of religious ideology, practice, or structure. It is a difficult exercise, and students are frequently shocked to realize that they can't identify many, if any, cultures completely free of religion. Try it. How many cultures and societies, ancient or contemporary, can you name that do not include some type of religious structure, even if it is foreign or unrecognizable as such from your vantage point?

When my students have finished struggling with this question, I ask them another: How has religion influenced you? Many of my students are quick to respond that they are not religious, grew up in a nonreligious family, and therefore have not been influenced at all by religion. Other students insist that even though they did grow up with some form of religion, they have since rejected it and are thus no longer under its potent sway. If pressed, you might offer a similar response to my students. But if you live in the United States, it is virtually impossible to avoid the influences of religion, regardless of whether you are a practitioner. At the very least, chances are that you regularly interact with someone who identifies as "religious." According to the Public Religion Research Institute's (PRRI) 2020 Census of American Religion, "Seven in ten Americans identify as Christian."[4] This means that not only do the majority of Americans identify as religious, but Christian values and ideologies permeate the religious landscape of American society.

A quick look at current news headlines, especially those focused on what is commonly referred to as the "culture wars," shows the scale of religion's influence over U.S. culture. Check out the news feed on your mobile phone and ask yourself how many of the issues currently debated in the public sphere, Congress, or the Supreme Court invoke religious ideology, practice, conviction, or belief. Pull a dollar out of your wallet and notice the phrase "In God we trust," which, by the way, was adopted as the official motto of the United States by an act of Congress in 1956. Recite the Pledge of Allegiance: "One nation under God, indivisible, with liberty and justice for all." Recall the last election cycle and ask yourself how many times you heard a political candidate refer to God, prayer, or faith.

My point is that very few, if any, of us completely escape the influence of religion. If we participate in cultural institutions, religion influences us. In the same way that religion played an important role in shaping how I understood the world growing up and consequently how I perceived disability, religion also influences larger cultural narratives about disability and ableism. Listening to what people with disabilities say about their experiences in religious communities and organizations, therefore, provides one important window into understanding the ubiquitous and problematic nature of ableism.

The problem of ableism matters for all of us. The fact that you've picked up this book makes it fairly likely that you live with a disability, care for someone with a disability, know a family member or friend with a disability, or have recently met someone with a disability. But even if none of these circumstances currently apply to you, they will at some point in your lifetime. Some disabled folks coined the phrase "TAB," which means temporarily able-bodied. TAB reminds all of us that good health and able bodies are tenuous states of existence that could change in a moment.

When I started writing this book, conversations about racial and gender diversity were becoming more commonplace in the public square thanks in large part to social movements such as Black Lives Matter and #MeToo. Even in that moment, unlike the current one where some elected officials are attempting to restrict public discussion about diversity, equity, and inclusion (DEI), disability was often left out of the conversation. On the thirtieth anniversary of the passage of the Americans with Disabilities Act (ADA), international disability rights activist Judith Heumann and former Department of Justice lawyer John Wodatch penned a *New York Times* opinion piece entitled "We're 20 Percent of America, and We're Still Invisible."[5] While Heumann and Wodatch celebrate the legal protections afforded to people with disabilities as a result of the passage of the ADA (and other similar legislative efforts), they also lament the disadvantaged status that people with disabilities continue to occupy in most arenas of society. Heumann and Wodatch make visible the ongoing invisibility of people with disabilities, observing that people with disabilities are still all too often relegated to the back of the proverbial line, whether in the workplace, educational settings, or the allocation of public goods such as fair housing and health care.

Memories of reports about the allocation of precious and limited health-care resources during the height of the COVID-19 global pandemic continue to haunt me. Various media outlets such as *The New York Times* and *The Atlantic* chronicled how hospital staff needed to decide which patients would receive limited hospital resources and beds. They determined who was and was not hooked up to a ventilator, who was and was not admitted to the hospital, and who was and was not treated for a virus that ravaged the world and killed millions of people. These were heart-wrenching decisions. Too often, in too many situations, people with disabilities were not hooked up to ventilators, were not admitted to the hospital, and were not treated for COVID-19. Too often, in too many situations, people with disabilities were relegated to the back of the line because their lives were deemed less worthy. Ableism is not a thing of the past. The passage of the ADA realigned some laws, but it did not eliminate ableist attitudes and practices.

Make no mistake: Ableism is a justice issue. I have chosen to explore ableism in the context of religious communities and organizations because, in a country where the majority of the population still purport to be religious, with all that this entails, it is shameful, if not sinful and immoral, not to care about ableism. Moreover, given the prevalence of religion in the United States, starting with religious institutions is as good and important a place as any to start raging against ableism. My hope is that whether or not you belong to a religious community, whether or not you are disabled, the following pages spark some self-reflection about the ways you participate in perpetuating ableism while also igniting a flame for engaging in the critical work of transformational disability justice. In short, I hope this book motivates you to join me in raging against ableism.

I don't remember a lot about the year between discovering that I could not read the chalkboard and receiving the diagnosis in Dr. Fall's office. I recall snapshots, but fifty years later, it is hard to know how much I actually remember and how much of what I think I remember comes from stories I have heard from my parents. Two memories that I know are accurate are what Dr. Fall said to me—that I could do anything—and the prayer warriors' intervention, that they laid hands on me and prayed for my healing. From my vantage point, a half century later, I now understand the stark difference between these two responses to my disability. The prayer warriors prayed for healing; they prayed that God would "cure" me. Their prayers were, of course, wrapped up in complicated understandings of what healing entailed or what it meant to be "cured." They mostly believed that their prayers had been answered because my diagnosis was the less bad of not great options. But their prayerful intervention sent a message to me that disability was undesirable, that it was something to ask God to eliminate.

Dr. Fall, in contrast, bestowed an incredible gift to me and my parents. In one brief sentence, he told us that my disability was not a tragic diagnosis; he told us that I was as capable and whole the day after the diagnosis as I was the day before; he told us that I could chase all my dreams and make them come true. Now that I am a parent, I marvel at how much my parents took his words to heart. I am amazed at how much freedom my parents gave me to test my wings and fly, especially when I was a teenager and young adult. They allowed me to try downhill skiing (I am still not sure how I made it work). They taught me to ride a bike and encouraged me to ride around the neighborhood. They supported me when I went to Germany during my junior year of college to study and travel through Europe. I know they worried about how I would do these things with limited sight, but they only ever made me feel like I could do anything I wanted to do.

I think a lot about the juxtaposition between the messages from the prayer warriors and Dr. Fall. Each message played a role in shaping who I am and how I move through the world. Each message arrived with its own set of complications. Many doctors are not as enlightened as Dr. Fall, and too many people receive the same message from medical professionals that I heard from the prayer warriors—disability equals tragedy. I am grateful for Dr. Fall's sage words; without them, I suspect my life might have been quite different. I am also grateful for the prayer warriors' well-intentioned care, however misguided. Unfortunately, from my conversations with interviewees and other disabled friends, I know that the prayer warriors' messages are more common than Dr. Fall's—particularly in religious communities. The rest of this book unpacks some of the most common and problematic messages people with disabilities receive from the "prayer warriors" in their lives. It also probes some of the underlying sources of these problematic messages and offers suggestions for how religious communities can begin to do the work of love and rage against ableism.

Religion is certainly not the only factor at the root of ableism, but as I peeled back the layers of my experiences with ableism, and as I asked other people with disabilities to peel back the layers of their own experiences, stories about religion and religious communities surfaced as some of the most significant experiences shaping feelings, attitudes, and perspectives on disability and ableism. Thus, this book uses the stories of people with disabilities, including my own, to reveal the insidious nature of ableism. I focus especially on the role religious practice, ideology, and communities play in cementing ableism as a largely unquestioned way of perceiving the world.

I began this project almost a decade ago, intending it to be a sociologically based academic study of the experiences of people with disabilities in religious communities and organizations. In that spirit, I set out to interview disabled folks, which I did.

When I started the project, I naively thought that I could write a book about the experiences of people with disabilities in religious communities that was not about me. I believed that I could simply acknowledge in the introduction that I, too, was a person with a disability and then move on, putting on my "objective" researcher hat and carrying on with writing a book with the requisite scholarly distance from my topic. The joke was most definitely on me!

The more I researched and wrote, the more the book reflected my experience. I have read many writers who say, "I cannot tell my story without telling other people's stories." I discovered that the reverse is also true: I cannot tell other disabled people's stories without also telling my story of living with a disability. So this book is about me, and it is also about other people with disabilities who agreed to talk with me about some of the most intimate, painful, wonderful, confusing, liberating experiences in their respective religious communities.

The interviews inform the content of the book, and I sprinkle excerpts from them throughout the text. While interviewees agreed to participate knowing that my end goal was to write a book, I use pseudonyms when referencing individual stories to protect their anonymity. I conducted semistructured, open-ended interviews, which means that I began with a list of questions but allowed the conversations to unfold organically. Interviewees belong to a variety of religious traditions, reside in all regions of the United States, and live with a range of physical disabilities. I issued a call through a variety of methods seeking participants with physical disabilities for a research study. I interviewed anyone who identified as a person with a physical disability.

I did not use a metric for determining whether participants fit a particular definition of disability; rather, I honored how each person identified and defined disability for themselves. To this end, my theoretical definition of disability is always at play with how the individuals discussed in the following pages understand disability. At times, my definition of disability aligns with how an interviewee defines disability, while at other times there are divergences in our respective conceptions of disability. I contend that celebrating all of the connections, contradictions, cohesions, and departures regarding definitions of disability allows us to gain a deeper understanding of the rich and diverse experiences of people with disabilities. Hence I do my best to allow multiple perspectives and definitions of disability to emerge throughout the book.

In addition to identifying as people with physical disabilities, all of my interviewees are over eighteen years old, and they all resided in the United States at the time of our interview. I did not interview people whose primary disability identification is an intellectual, cognitive, or developmental disability, nor did I interview parents or caregivers of people with disabilities. These are all critical voices for deepening our understanding of more general experiences of disability in religious communities, but due to the limitations of my project, I focus exclusively on the stories of people who live with physical disabilities as told in their own words.

Because interviewees volunteered to participate and because folks living in the intersections of multiple marginalized identity markers often find, for good reason, that telling their stories is potentially a risky and dangerous business, a shortcoming of the book is that my interviewees skew white, Christian, and cisgender. Hence I hope that this book sparks broader conversations about disability experience in religious communities. I imagine these conversations happening in all kinds of places and in all kinds of ways: among individuals, within specific religious communities, across wider denominational distinctions in singular traditions, and beyond the confines of particular religious boundaries in interreligious contexts. Moreover, I will count this project a success if it also sparks an expansion of broader literature that probes how disability experience informs the transformational work of disability justice.

Through candid storytelling, I ask you to notice the ableism around you and join me in raging against it. You will discover that some of these stories are painful retellings of destructive relationships that have turned the protagonists away from religious life and community. Other stories are tales of hope and discovery when it was thought that all was lost. Still other stories are less dramatic accounts of how regular people, faced with unusual circumstances, put together a life they deem worth living. All of these stories are windows into the sacred chaos, beauty, and resilience of the lives of people who inhabit bodies that do not always operate in the ways the larger, ableist society thinks they should.

~ 2 ~

Let's Talk About Disability

It surprises me how often people, strangers and friends alike, awkwardly inquire if they can ask me a personal question. I usually quip that they are free to ask, but depending on the nature of the question, I may not answer. Without exception, I always know what the nature of the question will be: It is always a question about my disability. I am happy to answer just about any questions my friends toss out about disability. Depending on the situation, I generally also answer strangers' questions, unless they require more than a one- or two-sentence answer. The questions I really dislike answering are the ones about how much or what I do and do not see. I loathe when someone holds up several fingers and asks, "How many fingers am I holding up?" Seriously—you're giving me an impromptu eye exam? No thank you. The impertinence of intrusive questions catches me off guard, and I used to be surprised about how awkward everyone feels about asking about disability, but I realized that the awkwardness stems from the very fact that the topic is complicated. Most able-bodied people don't know what to ask or how to articulate their questions.

What do I mean by the word "disability"? How do I determine who is and is not disabled? These questions vex anyone writing about disability because simple answers do not exist. There is no one universal experience of disability. Disability cuts across all other markers of identity, including gender, class, race, sexual orientation, and national and ethnic origin. The Centers for Disease Control and Prevention (CDC) estimates that sixty-one million, or 26 percent (one in four), of adults in the United States live with some form of disability.[1]

Disability can be obvious or hidden, physical or cognitive, mild or severe. Disaggregating the data about adults living with disabilities, the CDC reports that 13.7 percent have mobility disabilities (trouble walking or climbing stairs); 10.8 percent have a cognition disability (trouble concentrating, remembering, or making decisions); 6.8 percent have an independent living disability (trouble doing errands alone); 5.9 percent are deaf or have serious difficulty hearing; 4.6 percent have a vision disability, whether blindness or serious difficulty seeing even with glasses; and 3.6 percent have a self-care disability (trouble dressing or bathing).[2] Disability is simultaneously amorphous and ubiquitous, even when it is not explicitly apparent.

How do you define disability? I suggest doing the following exercise. Take a break from reading. Without thinking about it for too long, jot down your definition of disability. After you write down your definition, go back and review the words you used in your definition. Did you use neutral, negative, or positive descriptors for disability? Your answer likely depends on how much thought you've given to disability before picking up this book and how influenced you are by commonly held definitions of disability. Most people define disability as a physical or mental "lack" or "failure" of an individual body. According to this definition, disability leaves an individual disadvantaged, inevitably preventing them from enjoying a full and "normal" life. This definition of disability is solidly rooted in American neoliberal capitalist values such as rugged individualism, extreme independence, external success measured primarily through the ability to work and earn large amounts of money, and physical strength and prowess. It is the most common understanding of disability among able-bodied people.

Another common understanding of disability is what disability studies scholars refer to as the medical model, which also situates disability squarely in the lack or failure of particular individual bodies. The medical model is one of the earliest models asserted for understanding, thinking, and theorizing about disability. As the name suggests, the medical model is grounded in medical language and practice, following a protocol in which a credentialed expert identifies a pathology (disability), implements a treatment, and, ideally, eliminates or cures the initial pathology. For the medical model, the goal is always to eradicate disability, even if the cure is not always realized.

We can find a more neutral definition of disability in the language of the ADA, signed into law in 1990. The ADA defines a disabled person as "a person who has a physical or mental impairment that substantially limits one or more major life activities, a person who has a history or record of such an impairment, or a person who is perceived by others as having such an impairment."[3] As the first wide-sweeping civil rights disability legislation in the United States, the ADA "prohibits discrimination against individuals with disabilities in all areas of public life, including jobs, schools, transportation, and all public and private places that are open to the general public."[4]

For multiple reasons, the ADA represented an important cultural moment in the United States. Its passage culminated years of disability activism, finally granting people with disabilities a similar legally protected status as other minority groups. The law's passage also raised awareness about the experience of disability and ushered in a new era of public discussion of disability-related issues. And last but hardly least, the law initiated a subtle yet important shift in the collective imagination about the definition of disability. The ADA definition uses less toxic language than the medical definition, referring to disability as an "impairment" that limits some life activities rather than a lack or disadvantage for a particular body. The language of the ADA definition is primarily descriptive. It omits value-laden language that presents disability experience in monolithic and negative terms.

The ADA definition of disability aligns more closely with yet another model of disability: the social or, as some call it, the minority model.[5] Like the ADA definition, the social model starts with the neutral descriptor of physical impairment before asserting that disability results from unjust social structures and barriers. For example, a blind person is physically impaired because she cannot see, but she is disabled when reasonable accommodations are not made to ensure her equal and full access to printed material in school or at work. The social model insists that society, not individuals, bears responsibility for alleviating disabling conditions such as systemic discrimination, lack of access, and injustice.

While the social model expands the scope of the definition of disability, it has its own limitations. Some disability scholars note that the social model tends to gloss over the very real physical challenges of living with a disability. Feminist philosopher Alexa Schriempf highlights this tendency when she writes, "The social model, in focusing on the social construction of disability, has amputated disabled (especially women's) bodies from their impairments and their biological and social needs."[6] No amount of accommodation, for example, can mitigate extreme physical pain or fatigue, which may prevent a person's full participation. A danger of the social model is that a laser-like focus on the social construction of disability often inadvertently minimizes, or dismisses as irrelevant, the embodied experiences of disabled people.

Another shortcoming of the social model is that, in some iterations, it ignores how the definition of disability is embedded in complicated dynamics of social power and privilege. Scholars and people with disabilities alike argue that both the definition and the experience of disability are neither stagnant nor stable but rather porous and ever-changing. And since the definition of disability morphs over time, it follows that the definition of disability will be influenced or even dictated by the historical, cultural, and social factors in force at that time. So if the definition of disability changes and is determined by the people who are powerful and privileged at a given historical moment, we can deduce that the definition of disability gets tangled up in those systems of power and privilege. History, after all, gets told and recorded by those in power, by the winners and the privileged.

This is what we mean when we talk about systemic oppression, whether for disability or anything else: It is the assertion that systems of power and privilege, such as political and economic systems (e.g., capitalism), educational institutions, legal codes, or religious ideologies, wield disproportionate control over defining the realities of people with far less power and privilege. The social model recognizes that disability as a concept is socially constructed, but in its simplest form, it does not attend carefully enough to how the social construction of disability emerges out of power and privilege or how it places people with disabilities at a social disadvantage.

Throughout history, many people relied on religion and religious ideologies to make sense of disability. A few scholars (myself included) even use the somewhat contested language of "religious models of disability." An important thing to note when using religion to understand disability is that just as there is not a singular religion or religious worldview, there are multiple religious explanations for the presence of disability. Thus, it is most appropriate to refer to religious *models*, as opposed to the singular medical or social model of disability.

I include discussions of religious models in this book because many of my interviewees and their stories invoke religious models of disability, even if they do not use the precise language of religious models. Similar to the medical model, many of the more common religious models of disability that show up in the stories in this book situate disability as tragedy and as a failure of the individual body. Like the medical model, many religious models also prioritize eradicating disability, but they add an additional wrinkle to the causes and potential cures for disability. Religious models often invoke ideas such as "sin" or "karma"—concepts from Judaism, Christianity, and Islam and Hinduism and Buddhism, respectively—as causes of disability, as if taboo actions in this life, or a past one, result in physical punishments with divine origin. In these religious models, repentance, a more robust faith, or good karma (earned through correct action) provide necessary pathways to "cure." Many religious models, in other words, overlap with the medical model, but they also insist that some type of spiritual reckoning is required for a cure.

Plenty of ordinary people with disabilities, as well as scholars and activists, have noticed the problems with the most common models of disability (medical, social, and religious) and offered their own alternatives. One of my favorites comes from a feminist, queer, disability theorist named Alison Kafer, who in her book *Feminist, Queer, Crip* proposes a political/relational model of disability. Intersectional in nature, Kafer's political/relational model situates disability firmly in the realm of the political, foregrounds how systems of power determine how we understand disability, and emphasizes a desire for coalition building and collective imagining. The political/relational model simultaneously respects the specificity of critical theoretical frameworks while also calling for a relational political activism that includes disability as an equally informed site of subjective and critical knowledge production. In this way, the political/relational model attends to the lived realities of disability experience as well as to the power dynamics at play in constructing such categories as disability, gender, class, race, and so on. Moreover, Kafer's model insists that justice-oriented activist agendas are strongest when coalitions are formed among and between a variety of identity groups. For example, Kafer and other disability activist scholars write about "toilet justice," which involves people with disabilities and trans people working together to ensure that accessible and safe bathrooms are available in public spaces for everyone.[7]

Feminist disability theorist Rosemarie Garland-Thomson reflects the political/relational model when she asserts that feminist disability studies define disability as "a cultural interpretation of human variation rather than an inherent inferiority, a pathology to cure, or an undesirable trait to eliminate. In other words, it finds disability's significance in interactions between bodies and their social and material environments."[8] Garland-Thomson further distills the definition of disability as a "dynamic encounter between flesh and the material world."[9] She argues that it is the actual encounter between these two—flesh and world—that determines the extent to which an impaired body is disabled or not. By focusing on the encounter between body and world, Garland-Thomson remains attentive to both the embodied experience of physical impairment and how social and material environments produce or eliminate disabling conditions.

As should be clear by now: Defining disability is a messy undertaking. To state the obvious, everyone has their own idea about what disability is and is not. Even those of us who identify as disabled do not agree about what the term means. I align most closely with Kafer's political/relational model and with Garland-Thomson's definition of disability, both of which recognize that impairment is one form of variation and that disability is a function of the encounter between complicated bodies and the world. I contend, however, that no single model can fully capture the complex realities of disability. I resist most efforts to confine disability to a strict set of definitions or models that, more often than not, reduce it to a one-dimensional experience.

Most people with disabilities do not parse out their day-to-day experiences in terms of the differing models of disability. Nevertheless, the people I interviewed echoed the theoretical frameworks of one or more of the models of disability when they were reflecting on their experiences in religious communities. Many interviewees, for example, noted that their religious communities frequently offer prayer as a "cure" for disability: "If you pray hard enough, God will cure your disability." This seemingly supportive suggestion is embedded in both the medical and religious models of disability. Peeling the layers back reveals attitudes toward disability grounded in dominant cultural narratives of disability as tragedy and as something requiring elimination and cure. Other interviewees describe moments when their respective religious communities rallied to provide accommodations that would allow access to a previously unavailable physical space. In these examples, we see the social/minority model in action, in which people are rendered disabled when access is denied.

You will find strands of all of these models of disability in the pages that follow, but it is my hope that you will ultimately embrace a political/relational approach to addressing questions of access, inclusion, and equity. One of my aims is to help readers conduct an honest examination of when, where, and how they perpetuate one or more of the more simplistic and limiting models of disability and to help them understand that disability experience is far more complex than most medical, religious, or even social models capture. It is critical to notice how religious beliefs, practices, rituals, and texts implicitly or explicitly, intentionally or unintentionally, advance harmful models and definitions of disability. Understanding this is the first step toward rejecting negative attitudes and practices of disability, toward raging against ableism, toward realizing disability justice.

Another one of my aims is to explore avenues for wedding more disability-affirming religious models of disability with the political/relational model. While many of the stories in the following chapters reflect problematic religious models of disability, other stories reveal religious models that mirror the political/relational model's emphasis on intersectionality, coalition building, and collective imagining. If, as I argue in the previous paragraph, it is critical to notice how religious beliefs, practices, rituals, and texts implicitly or explicitly, intentionally or unintentionally, advance harmful models and definitions of disability, it is equally critical to notice where other religious beliefs, practices, rituals, and texts advance positive and life-giving definitions and models of disability. Identifying positive religious models is another important component of raging against ableism. Religious models of disability grounded in political/relational frameworks move us closer to realizing disability justice.

If defining what disability is or means is challenging, it follows that finding language to talk about disability is equally if not more challenging. Language and terminology evolve and change in response to cultural and historical shifts. As such, the ways we talk about disability and people with disabilities have also shifted over time.

A question my nondisabled friends often ask me is, "Do you prefer I describe you as a person with a disability or a disabled person?" In disabled circles, we call this question the people-first or identity-first language debate. One way to think about this debate is a disagreement over whether disability should be considered a defining part of a person's identity or simply one descriptor among many. Put another way: Am I a blind person, or a person who is blind? Person-first advocates argue that it is important to locate the person as the focus—for example, a person with autism or a person who is blind—because disability is just one aspect of identity. Person-first language emerged as one strategy for avoiding disability stigma, although there is disagreement about whether people-first language really makes a difference with respect to stigma. Identity-first language places disability first—for example, blind people or autistic people. Some disability activists prefer identity-first language, asserting that it signals disability pride.

Each camp—person-first or identity-first—argues that language choices are justice issues. On the one hand, supporters of people-first language maintain that this approach allows people with disabilities to claim the full spectrum of their various identities, which are not limited to their disability status. In other words, people-first language advocates assert that this approach is intersectional in nature. On the other hand, proponents of identity-first language assert that disability identity is something to celebrate rather than something to be sidelined or hidden.

I have no stake in the people-first or identity-first debate. In my writing and speaking, my practice is to tack back and forth between the two approaches. I do not believe that disability defines who I am (or who anyone with a disability is), and I am proud of my disability identity. As my friend and former commuter buddy, Billy, often says, two things can be true at the same time. I believe that each person should be able to speak about their disability in the fashion most comfortable and authentic to who they under-stand themselves to be. As such, I use both person- and identity-first language throughout the book.

Another language question that often comes up when talking with friends or family about disability is, What is the proper terminology to use when referring to someone who is disabled? Many folks rely on euphemisms for talking about topics that make them uncomfortable or with which they are unfamiliar. Phrases like "handicap," "special needs," "differently abled," or the one that most grates on my nerves, "differently challenged," are some of the most common euphemisms for disability. It is difficult to put into words the intensity of my repulsion to these phrases! Please stop using them; they come across as patronizing, demeaning, infantilizing descriptions of incompetent people. They do not accurately describe me or any of my disabled friends. Instead, ask us what we prefer.

If, for some reason, you need to describe someone's disability but cannot ask them how they like to be described, I suggest using the most neutral and accurate description. For example, "Darla is blind," "Charlie uses a wheelchair," or "Pat is disabled." Think of it this way: If you are asked to point someone out in a room, you would most likely use neutral language to describe some of their physical characteristics or what they are wearing—for example, "She is the woman with short brown hair who is wearing a blue shirt and gray pants." You would not use euphemisms or empty phrases. Why then do we do this with disability? I am blind; I am a disabled person. These are factual statements about me, and there is no reason to state them any other way. My blindness is not a big secret, and we do not need to pretend that it does not exist.

I wrote about the ubiquity of ableism in chapter 1. Language is perhaps one of the clearest examples of how ableism permeates culture and society. Ableist language is so pervasive that most of us, including those of us with disabilities, frequently do not realize we are using it. Take, for example, common phrases like "That is so lame," "It fell on deaf ears," "She is blind to the truth," "The city was paralyzed by the snowstorm," "He needed to step up and take responsibility," "She's crazy," and the list goes on and on. So many of the metaphors we use in daily conversation cast physical or mental traits or abilities in negative terms. Ableist metaphors and language leave those of us with bodies whose parts do not work in conventional ways feeling less-than and demeaned. As the philosopher Michel Foucault asserted, language shapes reality.[10] It is difficult not to internalize that blindness is a "bad" thing when I so frequently hear the word used as a metaphor for something negative or problematic in casual conversation. Ableist language is like racist and sexist language: It might be possible to shrug it off once or twice, but it is impossible to dismiss it when it's a constant barrage.

Try a thought experiment: Go back to the examples I cited in the previous paragraph and come up with nonableist phrases to express the same sentiments as the ableist examples. My guess is that you quickly came up with good alternatives without too much effort. If you're struggling with this exercise, here are some suggestions: "That is so lame / That is so problematic"; "It fell on deaf ears / No one paid attention, or they were not listening"; "She is blind to the truth / She refuses to acknowledge the truth"; "The city was paralyzed by the snowstorm / The city shut down because of the snowstorm"; "He needs to step up and take responsibility / He needs to take responsibility"; and "She's crazy / She's silly." It is usually not difficult to find an alternative to ableist language. What is more difficult is to train oneself, first, to notice and, second, to avoid using ableist language and metaphors. I am disabled, and I write and speak about disability, yet I catch myself relying on ableist language all the time. Avoiding ableist language and metaphors requires a conscious commitment. It also requires a willingness to admit when you make a mistake and to correct yourself. Avoiding ableist language is hard. To this end, I try my best not to use ableist language and metaphors in this book.

If I had written this book ten years ago, I probably would have said something different about my language preferences; ten years from now, I will most likely make different choices about disability terminology. What I find most important about the conversations around language and definitions of disability is not to establish, definitively, the "right" way to talk about disability. Rather, what is most important is that we continue to be in conversation about how language negatively and positively shapes our conceptions of disability and, as a consequence, how we treat or mistreat people with disabilities. This is why when my friends or strangers awkwardly inquire if they can ask me a personal question, I usually say yes. I don't have the absolute answer about what disability means, but I want to stay in conversation about definitions of disability and about the language I prefer.

~ 3 ~
Sinners, Saints, Supercrips, and Misfits

I travel a lot, either on my own or with my guide dog. Getting from one gate to the next in a bustling airport when you cannot see to avoid the hordes of people who pay no attention to their surroundings in their rush to their next flight, or when you cannot read the many signs directing you to the correct concourse, or when you cannot locate the bathroom or food court without help is challenging. Thus, I get assistance from airport employees to get where I need to go, just like unaccompanied minors or elderly people. Never mind that on more than one occasion, the handy assistants forgot about me and left me sitting at the gate while the door to my plane closed just as I realized their mistake. Or the fateful night when my assistant took me to the bowels of the airport and, without me noticing, swiped my wallet. My wallet arrived in my mailbox several weeks later, minus $250.

During one of my solo trips on the way to a professional conference, my airport assistant riddled me with blindness-related questions. Some of them landed just this side of intrusive. Because I'm at the mercy of the airport employees to reach my next gate, to pee, and to eat, I usually politely indulge their curiosity, even as I internally roll my eyes at their audacity. With a jolly tone and expressing genuine interest in my experience, this particular assistant fired her questions in rapid succession: How long have you been blind? How do you read? How do you match your clothes? How do you do your job if you can't see? Can you see anything? Do glasses help? Did you ever see normally? Etc., etc., etc. As I began to grow weary of her interrogation, we mercifully arrived at our destination. As she helped me find a seat in the gate area, she breezily imparted her concluding wisdom: "Honey, if you just pray hard enough, Jesus will forgive your sins and heal your blindness." As my blind eyes stared after her in stunned astonishment, the misguided evangelist dashed off to save her next unsuspecting disabled passenger.

Several years after my encounter with the airport evangelizer, I lay comfortably on my acupuncturist's table. As soothing music played quietly in the background and a warm, cozy blanket enveloped me, the acupuncturist gently inserted the tiny needles into my body. I love the tingly feeling I get when the needle goes in and then the feeling of sinking into a relaxed state of blissful half consciousness. But on this morning, just as I drifted into total oblivion, my acupuncturist quietly remarked, "You know, Chinese religion teaches that disability is the result of bad karma in a previous lifetime. It is a lesson that one's spirit needs to learn." Her sharp words yanked every part of my mind and body back into the room as she stabbed that inaccurate metaphorical needle into my heart. "Now," she said as she walked out the door, "just relax."

It astounds me how frequently able-bodied strangers, like my airport assistant and (former) acupuncturist, espouse their opinions about all things disability related as soon as they realize I am blind. I find it especially stunning when they authoritatively render judgment about the meanings and causes of disability. This occurs more frequently than you might imagine. A similar thing occurred when people (strangers and friends alike) found out I was pregnant:

Suddenly, everyone became an expert in parenting and could not control the urge to dispense their most sage parenting advice. For the record, I welcome helpful suggestions and advice when requested and, more importantly, when it's offered as support and not as a holier-than-thou decree. While the parenting advice came with plenty of recommendations about how to get babies to sleep through the night, the pros and cons (more often pros in my crowd) of breastfeeding, or what names were and were not appropriate to give a newborn, it rarely got tangled up with religious conviction. Strangers' commentaries on disability and its meanings and causes, in contrast, frequently arrive cloaked in religious ideology.

At the time of the airport and acupuncturist experiences, I felt all the feels. Recounting them here, years later, still sparks a strong visceral reaction. Not only did my airport assistant and acupuncturist spew inaccurate and, I would argue, dangerous theologies, but they judged me based on one detail about my life. They rendered their ugly verdicts, that I am a flawed, sinful person in need of internal repentance and external absolution. Yes, many Christians believe that if one prays enough, sins will be forgiven and healing (physical or spiritual) will occur. Yes, some practitioners of one or more of the various Chinese religions (my acupuncturist conflated multiple traditions into one) believe that the cause-and-effect laws of karma translate into retribution in one lifetime for deeds done in a past lifetime. A careful study of these respective religions—Christianity, Buddhism, Taoism, Confucianism—would reveal that these and other strangers have grossly oversimplified what the traditions actually say about disability and disabled people. Here's the rub, though: It does not matter that they were wrong. What matters is that they, and many, many other people, blithely impart their misinformed opinions.

Why does this matter? Because people like me—that is to say, people with disabilities—are constantly barraged with sentiments like these that wear us down to such an extent that we begin to believe that they are true. We start to internalize the idea that there is something "wrong" with us, that maybe, just maybe, my airport assistant and acupuncturist were right—maybe I am a sinner and disability is the consequence of my wicked past. Remember my confession about internalized oppression in chapter 1? This is an example of one of the many ways that it works. The real sucker punch is that when religious justifications wrap tightly around negative stereotypes, those of us raised in or affiliated with religious communities find them nearly impossible to ignore or dismiss.

Not all strangers accuse me of sin. I cannot tell you how often well-meaning people (either friends or strangers) tell me how much they admire me. Or how remarkable I am. These comments, too, are often tangled with religious ideology, particularly if they place me on a pedestal as some kind of saintly inspiration or example of courageous living. To be honest, if I had to choose one or the other—sinner or saint—I would choose the sinner. I am pretty sure sinners have more fun, and as sixteenth-century Protestant Reformer Martin Luther said, "Be a sinner, and let your sins be strong."[1] The fun factor aside, providing saintly inspiration is as exhausting as being cast as a hopeless sinner.

Writing about this takes me back to another airport and a different airport assistant—remember, I travel a lot! This time, my assistant banged on about how amazing I am because I am blind and still fly by myself. "You are such an inspiration to me," she declared. "I just admire you so much. God uses people like you to remind the rest of us how lucky we are." There are so many things to unpack in this airport assistant's assertions. To begin with, keep in mind that this woman knew me for about four minutes when she unequivocally declared my remarkableness. To her credit, she's not wrong: I am remarkable. But she lacked evidence to support her claims. All she knew about me was that I was blind and that I was able to do an activity (travel) that she apparently assumed blind people typically could not do, despite the fact that her job was helping disabled people move through an airport. The not-so-subtle message she communicated in her astonishment at my ability to fly by myself was that she had never considered this possibility and that if she had, she most definitely would have concluded that blind people could not travel alone. If they did, it represented a feat of unparalleled accomplishment.

I do not exist to remind this airport assistant—or anyone, for that matter—how "lucky" they are. I emphatically reject the belief that God uses me and my blindness to the benefit of others, especially as a walking, breathing, living reminder that their lives are somehow better than mine, more valuable, more worthy. I have a great life! I would not change it or trade it for any other. I want no part of a theology or God who uses one group of people and their particular identities to serve as inspirational reminders of how life could be so much worse for another group of people.

Ableism comes in many forms. Most people can probably rattle off a few examples of ableism without much effort: a building that does not have ramps or elevators, the lack of adequate resources and support for disabled children in educational settings, workplace discrimination against people with disabilities. These tangible examples are easy to recognize as ableism and ableist practices. Harder to pinpoint or recognize are ableist attitudes. These are the assumptions, presuppositions, or stereotypes we hold about people with disabilities, often without even realizing that they are ableist.

When I'm not indulging in strong reactions to the offensive attitudes expressed by strangers I encounter while just going about my business, I wonder where these ableist attitudes and ideas originate, how they manifest in the lives of people with disabilities, and how to disrupt their potent sway. Why is there often such a disconnect between the reality of living with a disability and the reality nondisabled people imagine for people with disabilities? Where do conceptions of people with disabilities as sinners or saints come from? How do these and other negative disability stereotypes get perpetuated and reinforced? What are some more positive—not to mention accurate—ways of thinking about or understanding disability and people with disabilities?

Early in my teaching career, I discovered the work of Black feminist sociologist Patricia Hill Collins. In her groundbreaking book *Black Feminist Thought: Knowledge, Consciousness, and the Politics of Empowerment*, Hill Collins asserts a theory of "controlling images," which I use to unpack some explanations for ableist attitudes and stereotypes. According to Hill Collins, controlling images are negative and stereotypical images and representations that produce, reinforce, and perpetuate the inequality through "interlocking" systems of racism, sexism, and classism.[2] Hill Collins specifically focuses on controlling images of Black women, such as the mammy, welfare mother, or hot mama, which provide ideological justification, on a cultural level, for the ongoing subordination and oppression of Black women. Hill Collins's analysis of how controlling images are leveraged by socially and culturally dominant groups, structures, and systems to define minoritized populations as the inferior and subordinate "other" can be applied to other marginalized groups. I spend a lot of time thinking about the controlling images of people with disabilities, especially those that produce, reinforce, and perpetuate the inequality of disabled people in religious communities.

Before we rush into borrowing Hill Collins's conception of controlling images and applying it to people with disabilities, however, we need to pause to consider the dangers of what Alison Kafer refers to as the "logic of substitution."[3] Hill Collins wrote about Black women; I am writing about people with disabilities. Kafer warns that swapping one social justice concept for another simply substitutes one set of cultural practices and assumptions for another. This simple substitution can diminish or even negate the power of the original theory—for example, by implying that experiencing ableism is the same as experiencing racism. One of the greatest dangers in doing this is that this substitution risks contributing to the all-too-common practice of erasing, often violently, the voices and experiences of Black women from theoretical realms of analysis and critique. Western scholars have practiced violent erasures such as these for millennia. It is the responsibility of white people not only to avoid but also to scorn the repetition of the death-dealing patterns of suppression, oppression, and silencing that Black women—indeed, all persons of color—are forced to endure. The responsibility is particularly heavy in a field like disability studies, which has been rightly and forcefully critiqued for its lack of attentiveness to how interlocking oppressions of race and class impact disability experience.

The logic of substitution may also imply, implicitly or explicitly, that the experiences of Black women (or of people of color generally) and those of people with disabilities are separate and distinct. It suggests that Black women are not disabled or vice versa. This is wrong. People of color and women in particular disproportionately live with some form of disability. According to the Centers for Disease Control and Prevention (CDC), one in four Black Americans is disabled, while one in five white Americans lives with disabling conditions.[4] Moreover, because women of color often have less access to adequate and affordable health care, they are thus at even higher risk of becoming disabled or experiencing more significant limitations because of disability. Because, as the social and political/relational models of disability remind us, disability is more than just the physical experience of impairment. Lack of access to adequate and affordable health care also adversely affects the extent to which living with a disability is disabling.

A solution to navigating the conundrum of the logic of substitution comes from critical race theorist, lawyer, and Columbia Law School professor Kimberlé Crenshaw's theory of intersectionality. In a 2017 interview, Crenshaw described intersectionality as "a lens through which you can see where power comes and collides, where it interlocks and intersects. It's not simply that there's a race problem here, a gender problem here, and a class or LGBTQ problem there. Many times that framework erases what happens to people who are subject to all of these things."[5] Intersectionality, in other words, argues that people's multiple identities must be considered at once, not separately.

Using an intersectional approach for exploring the controlling images of people with disabilities reminds us that our analysis is inadequate and true justice is not possible if we isolate our investigation to one group or component of identity and ignore the ways in which power and privilege collide, intersect, and interlock. Building coalitions and prioritizing the liberation of all who exist on the margins of society must be the goal of naming and disrupting the controlling images of any identity group. In using Hill Collins's concept of controlling images, I hope to expand the ongoing conversation of how controlling images function on structural levels in general to buttress systems of domination, power, privilege, and oppression for all who live on the margins.

I wish I could tell you that airport employees and acupuncturists hold the keys to an exclusive club when it comes to equating disability with sin. Unfortunately, this is not the case. Many of my interviewees shared similar stories in which they had been told that disability was somehow a result of sin. Whether in casual conversations with disabled friends or during the course of my interviews, the "sinner" came up over and over again as one of the most common controlling images of people with disabilities. The details differed from story to story, but the message was the same.

Max, a self-described retired Baptist minister in his early sixties, described many of the elements of the sinner controlling image as he told me his story. Max joked that "retired" was a bit of a misnomer, given that he maintained a busy schedule of preaching, teaching, and writing. By his late thirties, Max had a PhD, was working full time as a minister, and was, as he put it, "positioned to rise in denominational life." In the midst of his busy and by all accounts successful ministerial career, Max began having problems with detached retinas: "After three attempts [to repair the retina] in each eye, the doctors just kind of ran out of retina. I was totally blind from that point forward." Max's blindness stems from diabetic retinopathy, a complication of his long-term diabetes.

Max struggled with common questions after the onset of disability, asking "Why me?" and "I have all of these things on my résumé, but how am I ever going to use them anymore?" Bolstered by his faith, his church community, and a forthright nurse, however, Max transitioned from sight to blindness with relative ease. Recalling a pep talk from a nurse while he was in the hospital, Max described how he approaches his disability:

One of the nurses there, an African American woman, probably in her fifties, early sixties, came in one day when I was quite grumpy, and she gave me a good talking to. "God's not finished with you yet. You need to move beyond the things that have happened here and find what it is that God can use you to do." Concurrently with that, there was one of the most intense personal spiritual experiences that I can recall of sensing God's affirmation that "You need to know that you're the person that I created you to be. You just can't see anymore." And that has sort of been my motivating spiritual affirmation.

In a testament to how deeply his spiritual affirmation penetrates his life, not only did Max continue on his successful career path for the next twenty-plus years, but with an intrepid spirit, some creative ingenuity, and the help of friends and family, he also enthusiastically returned to water skiing—a sport he had loved as a sighted person!

Max's eventual positive and matter-of-fact attitude toward disability was not always matched by other members of his religious community. Steeped in the biblical literalism tradition of the Southern Baptist denomination, Max encountered folks who interpreted his disability as a negative sign or message from God: "I had a carload of ministers who had read a newspaper article about me show up at the office one day, and they wanted to come in and anoint me with oil and pray that my faith would increase so I could be healed of my blindness. My faith was obviously standing in the way of my healing." In extreme cases, a few people even linked Max's more "liberal" approach to theology with God's judgment and his disability: "Some people have thought that I should be able to understand that God is finished with me. My theology is different enough from the good ultraconservative Baptist upbringing they have [that they believe] this is God's way of making sure that I wouldn't be leading anybody astray with my terrible theology."

Max acknowledged that linking sin with disability was problematic and sometimes even hurtful, but on a personal level, he mostly dismissed such attitudes as misguided and uninformed. While Max gratefully noted that attitudes linking sin and disability were the exception in his circles and while Max also celebrated the positive alternative religious model of disability offered by his long-ago nurse, most of my interviewees reported encountering similarly negative attitudes linking sin and disability at some point in their own religious contexts. The basic script for all the stories from my interviewees followed remarkably similar patterns: "If you just pray hard enough, God will take away your sins, and you will be healed."

Two assumptions undergird the sinner controlling image. First, disability is always undesirable, and every effort should be made to eliminate it. Second, every cause of disability has an explanation, typically sin or past wrong deeds. These assumptions stem from the medical and religious models of disability that I referenced in chapter 2. As a reminder, these models operate on a very specific formula: identify the problem or pathology, implement a protocol, and eliminate or cure the problem. For the medical model, diagnosis, protocol, and cure rest securely in medical discourse and treatment. For problematic religious models, the so-called pathology also presents as a medical issue, but the underlying cause and subsequent treatment require spiritual correction rather than a mere resolution of physical symptoms. The linkage between spiritual health and physical well-being means that while the "cure" for some religious models might include medical intervention, it also always involves spiritual realignment, often taking the form of repentance for past deeds (i.e., sin) and prayer. If a "cure" actually does result, it presumably includes forgiveness from God for said past deeds.

In medical and problematic religious models, disability resides squarely in the individual impaired body. Both define disability as a limit or lack in a specific body that, for whatever reason, does not function in the way deemed "normal." And because some religious models include a spiritual and moral lack or failure, they also include a hope for "fixing" the impaired body via some combination of medical intervention and spiritual healing. Harkening back to my acupuncturist, let's consider the Buddhist and Hindu theories of karma, which demonstrate the logic of individual responsibility for explaining disability. Karma, meaning action, follows the law of cause and effect: For every action, there is a subsequent reaction or consequence. Good actions or deeds yield positive consequences, and bad actions or deeds render negative outcomes. According to this overly simplistic understanding of the logic of karma, performing enough good deeds in this lifetime should ensure future lifetimes free from disability. Let me hasten to add that the concept of karma is more complicated than this, but this is often how it is explained, especially by Westerners who are neither Buddhist nor Hindu.

For many Christians, the spiritual reckoning that would eliminate disability involves acknowledging and atoning for one's wrongdoings or sins. As I think, write, teach, and speak about religion and disability, I often wonder why so many Christians adhere to a problematic religious model and equate the presence of disability with sin. Of course, there are no simple answers to my musings, but the more I wonder about this, the more I notice how the healing stories of Jesus in the Christian Gospels portray disability. If you are disabled, reading about Jesus's healing miracles may leave you feeling like there is not much room for you in the Kingdom of God.

One could write a whole book examining the portrayal of disability in the Christian Gospels—and, in fact, some scholars have! Here, I focus on two healing stories that I have written about elsewhere and that demonstrate how the average Christian churchgoer may erroneously conclude that disability represents sin. Let's start with the story of the man born blind in the Gospel of John. In John 9, Jesus restores sight to a man who was born blind by spitting on the ground to make mud, spreading the mud on the blind man's eyes, and instructing him to wash the mud off in a pool. When the blind man returns from rinsing off the mud, his sight is restored, and the people who knew him as a blind man are astonished. Throughout the conversations following the miracle, the text draws metaphoric, symbolic, and literal linkages between the state of being blind and living in darkness and spiritual ignorance, on the one hand, and between physical sight and the ideas of living in light and spiritual insight, on the other. "Jesus said, 'I came into this world for judgement so that those who do not see may see, and those who do see may become blind.' Some of the Pharisees near him heard this and said to him, 'Surely we are not blind, are we?' Jesus said to them, 'If you were blind, you would not have sin. But now that you say, "We see", your sin remains'" (John 9:39–41).[6]

I cowrote an article about this story of the man born blind with my friend and biblical studies scholar Jennifer Koosed. In that article, Jennifer and I note, "In John 9, the physical condition of blindness always also connotes metaphorical blindness as a mental or spiritual condition, or ignorance. Both the literal and metaphorical meanings of blindness are always present every time the words 'blind' and 'to see' are used in the story."[7] Questions that the disciples ask Jesus about the blind man when they first encounter him at the outset of the story prepare the reader for the lessons to come: "His disciples asked him, 'Rabbi, who sinned, this man or his parents, that he was born blind?'" (John 9:2). Jesus's response to the disciple's question regarding whose sin caused the man's blindness prevents an overly simplistic interpretation of the passage: "Neither this man nor his parents sinned; he was born blind so that God's works might be revealed in him" (John 9:3). While some scholars have argued that Jesus's answer to his disciples' question disrupts the linkage between sin and disability, the dominant metaphor remains: Those of us who are blind do not—or worse, *cannot*—have "spiritual sight." This story, like the other healing miracle stories found in the Christian Gospels, implies that bodies that are disabled must be made physically "whole" before those who inhabit them can be made spiritually whole.

Consider another example of Jesus's healing magic from the Gospel of Mark. In Mark 2:1–12, Jesus heals a paralytic man from Capernaum. The rough sketch of the narrative goes like this: Jesus is preaching and teaching and draws a crowd. A paralyzed man and his four friends go to hear Jesus, but they can't get into the house because the crowd is so large. The friends get creative and decide to cut a hole in the roof (as one does when the doorway is crowded) through which they lower the paralyzed man and his mat. Jesus notices the paralytic and his friends, probably due to their dramatic entrance. Jesus announces that the paralyzed man's sins are forgiven because of his friends' faith. The Jewish authorities challenge Jesus's authority to forgive sins. Jesus then proclaims that the paralyzed man is healed and tells him he is healed. Jesus tells the Jewish authorities that it is easier to forgive sins than to heal a paralytic man, proclaiming that if he can do the harder thing, heal, he can do the easier thing, forgive sin.

Fun fact: The one time in my life that I preached a sermon (be assured, I am not a preacher), I used this story. Like any good sermon preparer, I went to the biblical commentaries, which are written by scholars who are considered experts in biblical interpretation. The commentaries assert that the question of Jesus's authority is what is at stake in this story. The scribes and Pharisees challenge Jesus's claims that he can forgive sins, claiming that only God holds that power. They are irritated that Jesus is doing things that only God can do. According to the commentaries, Jesus resolves the tension, at least in his mind, and "proves" his authority by healing the paralytic man. For Jesus, the healing of the paralytic man is kind of a stick-your-tongue-out, "take that" moment with the scribes and Pharisees because he had done the hard thing, healing, which means that he can certainly do the easy thing, forgiving sin. Hence according to the commentaries, Jesus settles the question of his authority.

The commentary and the traditional interpretation of Mark's story irk me. I have no real beef with Jesus proving his authority to the scribes and Pharisees. What I find problematic is that he uses the erasure of disability to do it. And if that is not annoying enough, Mark, like John in the first narrative, also links sin with disability because—if you read carefully—disability disappears in conjunction with forgiving sin. Take a moment to think about how

John's and Mark's stories might sound to someone with a disability, especially one who does not anticipate miraculous healing anytime soon.

The erasure of disability is not unique to the Christian Gospels of John and Mark. Every time Jesus encounters disability in the Christian Gospels, he heals it. The implicit and frankly explicit message in the healing stories is that people with disabilities do not get into the Kingdom of God with their disabilities—first, they must be healed. Jesus never commends the faithfulness of a person inhabiting a disabled body; he only extols faithfulness after, or simultaneous to, healing. As Australian disability advocate Elizabeth Hastings writes in a quote I love to use in my writing and speaking, "With all the respect due to the ten lepers, the various possessed, and the sundry blind, lame, and deaf faithful of scripture, I reckon people who have disabilities may have been better off for the last two thousand years if our Lord had not created quite so many miraculous cures but occasionally said, 'your life is perfect as it is given to you—go ye and find its purpose and meaning,' and to onlookers, 'this disability is an ordinary part of human being, go ye and create the miracle of a world free of discrimination.'"[8] Why, we might ask, given his insistence on accepting the "least of these" with all their imperfections, does Jesus never simply welcome a person with a disability into the community of believers just as they are?

I preached the previously mentioned sermon on the healing of the paralytic man during a chapel service at a small Christian college. I asked the congregants to think carefully about what the story about the paralytic man said and how it might come across to a person with a disability. I asked listeners to wrestle with what it would mean for Christians to allow the possibility of spiritual sight to those who cannot see. I sat with the college chaplain at the community dinner following the service and my sermon. We chatted through dinner about how much she liked what I said and how I made her think differently about the story. Toward the end of the meal, she jokingly thanked me for filling up her calendar for the next few days because she'd be hearing from a lot of students who would want to process my sermon. My first thought was that the students were so blown away by my brilliant and insightful interpretation of the healing of the paralytic from Capernaum story that they would need a space to rethink their ideas about disability and the problematic aspects of the healing miracles. But as she kept talking, it became apparent that the chaplain expected to hear from students upset that I critiqued Jesus.

I cannot lie: I was disappointed to hear that she thought students' takeaway from my sermon would be a critique of their almighty Jesus rather than a critique of how that same Jesus always eradicated disability. To be sure, the biblical canon only includes snapshots from the historical Jesus's life; we do not know everything he did and said. It is possible that there were instances when Jesus did welcome people with disabilities into the community without first healing them but that those accounts did not make it into the Gospels. What we do know for sure is that, where the canonical text is concerned, Jesus's response to the disabled people he encounters is to "fix" them and showcase their cured bodies as evidence of great faithfulness, suggesting that disabled bodies are less faithful.

It should be said that many Christians with disabilities find hope and inspiration in these healing stories. Moreover, the biblical text includes other examples of individuals with disabilities who were elevated as spiritual leaders, including Moses, Jacob/Israel, and St. Paul. There are, in other words, multiple moments where the biblical text muddles the idea that disability must be eliminated for a person to have significant spiritual insight. Nevertheless, while many of my interviewees reported that they had received contradictory and sometimes confusing messages about these biblical healing stories, almost all of them had been told at least once, typically by someone in their faith community, that if they had enough faith or just prayed hard enough, Jesus would take away their sins and heal their disability. Even as scholars and disability rights activists have challenged a simplistic understanding that disability equals sin, my interviews and own experience demonstrate that these oversimplified interpretations of disability continue to be communicated and carried away from the Christian pulpit.

The ubiquity of healing stories in the Christian Bible and, more broadly, in American life goes a long way toward explaining how controlling images such as the sinner become so ingrained in non-disabled people's understanding of disability. Even more troubling, however, is that many people who are disabled also often absorb these same messages about sin, karma, and disability. They internalize the belief that to be disabled is to be a sinner. In these ways, the controlling image of the person with a disability as a sinner oozes in and through religious communities, cementing ableist assumptions, attitudes, and beliefs. Is it any wonder, then, that random strangers feel free to surmise that because I am blind, I am a sinner?

Whenever I talk about the sinner and saint controlling images of people with disabilities, someone inevitably remarks that they would prefer to be identified as a saint rather than as a sinner. I've already admitted that I think sinners have more fun, but, of course, one of the points of controlling images is that we do not choose them for ourselves. And in practice, nondisabled people are much more likely to ascribe the inspiring saintly status to me than the faithless sinner. At least that's what they'll tell me to my face.

The saintly attribution comes in many forms, most often delivered by a friend, family member, or colleague going on and on about how amazing I am. It is 100 percent clear to me that comments like these are always intended as compliments, and I usually receive them as such. At the same time, when these remarks are in response to or connected to my disability, they feel complicated and loaded to me. On the one hand, I do not need or want the pressure that accompanies living a saintly life. On the other hand, while masked under the veneer of a compliment, they communicate a level of discomfort with disability that comes across as patronizing and rooted in pity. When coupled with religious ideology, these compliments are often outright offensive.

These accolades are especially hard to reconcile when they come from beloved friends or family members. I remember sitting at the island in one of my aunt's kitchens sometime during high school. I was keeping her company while she cooked, and I waited for one of my cousins to come home. I have a large extended family—my dad has ten siblings and my mom has four. In total, I have fifty-five cousins. Most of them live in southern Ontario, but my dad's oldest brother's family moved to the same town where we lived in Indiana. Growing up, I spent as much time at their house as I did at my own. So to say that the aunt whose island I sat at is my favorite would be unfair because they are all my favorites for different reasons. But it is fair to say that she was the aunt with whom I spent the most time and knew the best.

I don't remember everything we talked about that day, but I vividly remember my aunt telling me that she thought I was a special young woman. She told me that she was amazed by the way I handled my vision loss and that she thought God had special plans for me. I can't recall her exact words, but the spirit of her comments was that she was proud to be my aunt and that she was inspired by my cheery can-do attitude. Oh yeah, and although she didn't quite state it outright, that in all of this, I was a good Christian example for my friends and family.

Even remembering that exchange now, memories of love and support from that aunt flood over me. To this day, I know that while she was alive, she was one of my biggest champions. I know she harbored no ill intent in her comments—quite the opposite. But comments like that, even when wrapped in love, leave me with a complicated set of emotions that are hard to explain. I appreciate the admiration, but it makes me feel like I can't admit when I feel angry and frustrated about my disability. I am glad people find me inspiring, but it makes me feel like I must always live up to their expectations. I am happy that there are folks in my life who think I am special (although I really hate that word), but it makes me feel like I am somehow different and set apart from everyone else. My responses to the saintly label tangle up with conflicting emotions that don't make sense to most of my able-bodied friends. When I try to explain, something always gets lost in translation.

Many of my interviewees echoed similar sentiments about how it made them feel when friends, family, and members of their respective religious communities elevated them as saintly exemplars. For example, Jessica is a mom in her early thirties with two young children whom she was homeschooling at the time of our interview. Diagnosed with lupus, a chronic autoimmune disease, in her late twenties, Jessica had left her high-pressure, fast-track career to minimize the stressors that exacerbated her illness. Soon after the lupus diagnosis, Jessica's doctors conceded that she could try to have a much-wanted second baby. Early in her subsequent pregnancy, Jessica became extremely ill. "Not like typical morning sickness," Jessica told me. "I mean, I couldn't even keep water down. I was just always dizzy and weak. It got so bad to the point where I couldn't walk, I couldn't speak without slurring. And I was hospitalized on and off for six weeks, and they couldn't figure out what was wrong with me—why my blood pressure was so low, why I was so weak, why I couldn't keep anything down with even the best antinausea drug."

When Jessica genuinely believed that death was the only possible outcome, she found a new doctor. After running a few tests and reviewing her symptoms, he diagnosed her with Addison's disease—a condition in which the adrenal glands do not produce enough cortisol and aldosterone. Addison's disease was causing Jessica's body to attack itself, severely impeding the functions of her heart, kidney, and other major organs. The new doctor immediately prescribed steroids. Within hours, Jessica was sitting up, talking, and eating Jell-O! Two days later, she went home from the hospital. Jessica noted that there is no apparent connection between lupus and Addison's disease but that it is not unusual for someone with lupus to develop additional health complications. She delivered a healthy, full-term baby several months after the diagnosis.

At the time of our interview, Jessica and her husband attended an interdenominational church where her husband served on the ministerial staff. For Jessica, religion and God did not become personally meaningful realities until she was forced to confront her own mortality and subsequent life with a chronic condition. But while faith and illness are inextricably intertwined for Jessica, church and illness are not. Jessica regularly attends church, and it is an important aspect of her life, but she noted that most days she prefers to hide her health challenges from her church community. Jessica sheepishly admitted that, to a certain extent, this is about pride and vanity, but the main reason she conceals her illnesses is that she does not appreciate the reactions her disabilities elicit. Other people typically minimized their own struggles in the face of Jessica's challenges, but more troubling were the people who expressed admiration or described her as an inspiration. "It's really odd for someone to say to me, 'Oh, you're so strong. I don't know how you do it.' I don't like hearing it," Jessica emphatically said, "because I don't have a choice. Kind of strange. And I don't like to be put in that place where people look to me as an example because I do things wrong all of the time, and I don't need that kind of pressure." Jessica vehemently rejected the ways in which her church friends attributed saintlike qualities to her. The saintly expectations added stress to an already stressful reality, and she did not feel as though she deserved the accolades.

Ella, another one of my interviewees, almost burst through the phone with her energy and zest for life. She told me about her experiences in a variety of religious communities, from growing up in a Reform tradition, to attending a Christian school, to worshipping briefly in a Jewish synagogue, to finding a home in an Episcopal church. Ella was born with cerebral palsy (CP), which the CDC describes as "a group of disorders that affect a person's ability to move and to maintain balance and posture."[9] The symptoms vary from person to person, but at its core, CP results from damage to the developing brain that makes it difficult to control muscles. Ella echoed many of Jessica's comments about her frustrations with being put on a pedestal by her Christian friends:

> Even before I was able to articulate that, like, I would sit around with these friends of mine in high school, and we would talk

about how annoyed we were that people would think that, you know, we were all of a sudden these super-Christians because we go about living our lives, right? But that sort of . . . looking back, that really sort of set off something for me. It's like I became really aware, I think, during that time that . . . that Christians in particular look at me and they . . . they, you know, more often than not, they assume that I'm some sort of saint.

Why do religious communities, and especially Christian folks, tend to ascribe saintly status to people with disabilities? The work of Christine James, who writes about Catholicism and disability, introduced me to the concept of "moral ecology,"[10] which has helped me sort out some answers to this question. James explains moral ecology as "an understanding that the ethical context of a community often influences the ethical behavior of individuals and that institutions have a moral imperative to create the proper moral ecology for their members."[11] In this spirit, religious communities seek moral exemplars who bolster the moral ecology of their community. Throughout the history of Christianity, and especially in the Catholic Church, saints provided the moral examples for the moral ecology of their respective contexts.

What I find fascinating about stories of saints is that so many of their biographies include descriptions of overcoming disability—physical or cognitive—or of having a special relationship with God because of their disability. Whether or not these stories are historically verifiable, many of them describe intense physical or psychological suffering that historically granted saints a holy, sacred, and elevated status but today reads as disability. Fast-forward to some late twentieth- and early twenty-first-century statements from the United States Conference of Catholic Bishops and the Vatican Committee for the Jubilee Day, and notice the language they use in discussing people with disabilities:

They [people with disabilities] bring with them a special insight into the meaning of life; for they live, more than the rest of us perhaps, in the shadow of the cross. And out of their experience they forge virtues like courage, patience, perseverance, compassion, and sensitivity that should serve as an inspiration to all Christians.[12]

Disability is not a punishment; it is a place where normality and stereotypes are challenged, and the Church and society are moved to search for that crucial point at which the human person is fully himself [*sic*]. This paper aims to help discover that the person with disability is a privileged interlocutor of society and the Church.[13]

While neither of these quotations explicitly states that people with disabilities are saints, they ascribe a similar "privileged," "special," and "inspirational" saintlike status to people with disabilities.

Religious communities additionally elevate both saints and people with disabilities as holy exemplars for the ways in which they nobly suffer. In the same ways that accounts of historical saints typically include detailed descriptions of physical or psychological suffering, many contemporary able-bodied people assume that people with disabilities experience literal physical or psychological suffering. Some do, some don't, but that's not the point. Unlike the sinner controlling image, the saint controlling image does not equate disability with sin or punishment. But like the sinner, the saint also assumes that disability always equals suffering. In the sinner controlling image, suffering through disability reveals the presence of sin; in the saint controlling image, suffering through disability produces holy or moral exemplars.

Although he uses slightly different language to describe it, Ibrahim, a Muslim man with multiple sclerosis (MS) in his forties, echoed a similar understanding of saintliness during our interview. Ibrahim rejected the notion that disability signifies a sinful character. According to his interpretation of Islam, disability is just one of many "tests" required of humans in this lifetime. People who are tested the most are also the most admired. "Islamically speaking, people who are tested a lot are actually revered. They're saying, 'Wow, God must really think highly of you. Because they say the people who are tested the most—and this is also biblical, this is the Torah, this is in the Qur'an—were prophets.'" Ibrahim went on to assert that God loves prophets the most and that God gives the hardest tests to the people who can handle them. "God knows that there's something in you that is above everybody else. Honestly, that's how we're taught in Islam about how you look at disability." Muslims are instructed through the Qur'an to emulate all prophets, with the Prophet Mohammed, the founder of Islam and believed to be the greatest prophet of all, as the supreme model.

Thus, patterns begin to emerge across religious lines of people with disabilities being elevated as inspirational models of holy and exemplary living. They hold a privileged and special status in their respective religious communities. At first glance, there is something appealing about being "revered" or set apart as "special," especially when this places you in God's highest favor. Yet most of my interviewees emphatically rejected this interpretation of disability. As Jessica explained earlier, it's a lot of pressure to be cast as inspirational. And there's a flip side as well. If your ability to deal with your disability inspires others, that doesn't leave a lot of room for struggle. People who know they're seen as inspirational saints feel as though they cannot show weakness, even if this is not true. Functioning as a saint or moral exemplar bears a heavy burden. The logic of ableism sets people with disabilities apart from their able-bodied counterparts. The distinction is oppressive, whether it happens because one is perceived as a damaged sinner or an exemplary saint.

There are days when I want to scream that it is hard as hell to live with a disability. On those days, I must be honest that I think you're damn right when you think I'm a saint. This is one of the many paradoxes I struggle with as a disabled person. Disability can be challenging; for many people, disability is nothing but challenging. I struggled more to complete a PhD than most of my friends who could just pick up a book and read, search the library stacks to find the text they needed, or skim a chapter to find the needed quote they remembered reading but forgot to write down. It was harder for me to parent a toddler who dashed around the house, picking up things to stick in his mouth that might have been dangerous, but that I did not notice because I could not see him. It broke my heart to not be able to plop my son on my lap and simply read a book to him. It is harder for me to get to and from work because I cannot drive myself; I must rely on the whims of other people's schedules. I end up with more goose eggs on my head than most people (unless you are a total klutz—you know who you are) because I bang into walls and doorjambs when I'm not using a cane or guide dog.

So, yes, I am flipping amazing. I am straight up remarkable. I do work harder than most people to do some of the most mundane tasks. I want you to notice this about me, and at the exact same time, I want you to think I am just another regular person doing what regular people do. I can't explain the paradox; it is just my truth. I know this is confusing for my friends and family because I say one thing on one day and a completely different thing on the next day: Revere me as a saint; stop revering me as a saint!

The supercrip, a concept I mentioned in the first chapter, is similar to the saint controlling image, but it emerges out of the disability community and has no religious underpinning. The saint and supercrip controlling images both extol and admire people with disabilities by holding them up as inspirational beacons. But the supercrip departs from the saint because it divides people with disabilities into categories of the typical disabled and the hyperable disabled. Emphasizing hyperability as the sign of a "good" or even the "best" kind of person with a disability, the supercrip may be the most insidious controlling image because it blends the assumptions that disability equals suffering and that disability must be overcome with the cultural trope of the physically aberrant hero. Disability studies scholars Jared Goggin and Christopher Newell describe the supercrip this way: "Those 'suffering' with disability, according to this cultural myth, need to come to terms with this bitter tragedy, and show courage in heroically overcoming their lot while they bide their time for the cure that will come. The protagonist for this script is typically the 'brave' person with disability; or, as this figure is colloquially known in critical disability studies and the disability movement—the supercrip."[14]

One of the best descriptions I have heard or read of what it means to be a supercrip comes from queer disability activist and writer Eli Clare. If you have not read his books, go find one as soon as you are finished with this one! In his memoir, *Exile and Pride*, Clare begins a description of his experience as a supercrip with commentary on the broader phenomenon:

> A boy without hands bats .486 on his Little League team. A blind man hikes the Appalachian Trail from end to end. An adolescent girl with Down's syndrome learns to drive and has a boyfriend. . . . The nondisabled world is saturated with these stories: stories about gimps who engage in activities as grand as walking 2,500 miles or as mundane as learning to drive. They focus on disabled people "overcoming" our disabilities. They reinforce the superiority of the nondisabled body and mind. They turn individual disabled people, who are simply leading their lives, into symbols of inspiration.
>
> I've been a supercrip in the mind's eye of nondisabled people more than once. Running cross-country and track in high school, I came in dead last in more races than I care to count. I ran because I loved to run, and yet after every race, strangers came to thank me, cry over me, tell me what an inspiration I was. To them, I was not just another hopelessly slow, tenacious high school athlete but a supercrip, tragic brave girl with CP, courageous cripple. It sucked. The slogan on one of my favorite T-shirts, Black cotton inked with big fluorescent pink letters, one word per line, reads PISS ON PITY.[15]

The burden of being a saint or supercrip is cumbersome indeed. As Jessica observed earlier, these controlling images put a lot of stress and pressure on disabled people. You feel like you always have to put on a brave face and that you can never complain, even when you are justified in doing so. For many people with disabilities, the combination of serving as a community's moral exemplar, being valorized as a saint, and being expected to rise above disability and outperform both one's disabled counterparts and nondisabled people is exhausting at best and soul crushing at worst.

One of my cousins asked me once, after reading a much earlier version of this chapter, why it bothered me so much to be admired by people who know and love me. It's a good question, and you will not be surprised when I say yet again that the answer is complicated. While on the surface, the sinner controlling image seems to reside at the opposite end of the spectrum from the saint and supercrip controlling images, the damaging and exclusionary consequences embedded in all three of these images are remarkably parallel. I identify four "problematic parallels," as I call them, which partly answer my cousin's question.

First, whether the able-bodied cast people with disabilities as sinner, saint, or supercrip, their understanding of disability is that it dwells squarely in the impaired body. None of these controlling images takes seriously the complex constellations of social and cultural conditions that contribute to experiences of exclusion, discrimination, and lack of access. For them, disability is always and only deficiency in the individual body, illustrating some combination of the evidence of wrongful behavior, the demonstration of noble suffering, or the marvel of heroic overcoming. Regardless of the specific controlling image, disability is always cast as an isolated, individually embodied experience. Because disability is understood as a "failure" of the individual body, the emphasis is on "fixing" bodily impairment instead of confronting structures of discrimination and oppression.

Second, whether portrayed as evidence of sin, sainthood, or hyperability, disability sharply denotes a distinct other, marking clear boundaries between "us" and "them": able-bodied and disabled. The sinner controlling image perpetuates the us/them dichotomy through both negative and positive reinforcements. On the one hand, the disabled body issues a warning to able bodies about what can happen if you sin. On the other hand, the disabled body affirms that you are not a sinner because you are not disabled. In these ways, the controlling image of the sinner subtly yet powerfully flags disabled bodies as embodied reminders of what happens when you screw up (read: disability) as well as evidence that you have not screwed up too much, at least not enough to warrant disability.

In a similar vein, the saint and supercrip controlling images reassure people with able bodies that only those who can "handle" disability are actually "afflicted." Using somewhat convoluted logic, the saint and supercrip controlling images allow able-bodied folks to feel humbly superior through what they convince themselves is weakness: "I do not have the strength to do what you do. I am too weak to handle a disability . . . thank goodness—lucky me." This misguided logic continues, "I do not possess the psychological fortitude to be either saint or hero, and thus I surely will never be disabled." To these folks, I always want to retort in my sweetest, most condescending tone, "Bless your heart, you are right. You are not as strong, amazing, or wonderful as I am, so you most definitely could not handle disability with my flair, wit, and aplomb!"

As Edward Said articulated in his formative theory of Orientalism, the dominant group's ability to define itself against an/other is a central way that these groups subordinate and dominate these others.[16] The presence of an inferior other is always necessary for establishing one's own privileged status. Thus, the sinner, saint, and supercrip controlling images of disabled bodies, having become fully "othered," allow the nondisabled to rest comfortably in their spaces of able-bodied privilege: Disability happens to those who either deserve it or can handle it (the other), and from my able-bodied privilege, I can safely say that neither of those statements describes me. Disabled sinners, saints, and supercrips bear the markers against which an able-bodied status quo is defined and measured.

Third, whether the narrative of disability relies on the controlling image of the sinner, saint, or supercrip, it assumes that disability is synonymous with suffering and therefore undesirable.

Physical cure is always the goal. Explicit statements like "If you pray hard enough, your sin will be forgiven, and you will be healed" leave no room for interpretation—disability should be eradicated. The equation is simple: Sin causes disability, repentance atones for sin, forgiveness follows sincere repentance, and forgiveness results in cure.

The narrative of disability as undesirable for the saint controlling image is, however, more implicit. A common motif in many stories of saints—historic or contemporary—is that disability is one's "cross to bear." The language of cross-bearing harkens directly back to the biblical story of Jesus's crucifixion. In the Gospel of John, Jesus carried his own cross to the site of execution.[17] The thinking implicit in the saint imagery is that, in the same way that Jesus suffered, people with disabilities suffer, but also like Jesus, they will be rewarded for their suffering at some future time. People with disabilities will get their reward—their cure—in heaven.

Fourth, all of these scripts, whether based on the sinner, the saint, or the supercrip, ultimately elicit a response of pity from the able-bodied. As I already noted, most people find it more desirable to be thought of as an inspirational saint or supercrip who evokes compassion than to be cast as a sinner, breeding contempt. But in this case, compassion and contempt are the parasitic twins of pity. It is impossible to be equal to someone who pities you. Moreover, the object of pity, rooted in both contempt and compassion, is perceived as weak, inferior, and subordinate. Stuck in the cycle of pity, the sinner, saint, and supercrip controlling images ultimately buttress an able-bodied norm and privilege, thereby cementing ableism in the collective imaginary.

Have you ever had the experience where you read something that completely reorients your thinking? This happened to me when I first read one of my favorite feminist disability theorist's articles, "Misfits: A Feminist Materialist Disability Concept."[18] In the essay, Rosemarie Garland-Thomson proposes the term "misfit" for rethinking disability. There's a lot I love about this article, but what I keep returning to in my writing and speaking is that fitting and misfitting are determined through the "dynamic encounter between flesh and world."[19] When two things come together in harmony, there is a fit, but when they are discordant, there is a misfit. Garland-Thomson uses the example of trying to put a square peg into a round hole to describe the concept. There is nothing inherently wrong with either the peg or the hole; they just don't fit.

Where the theory of misfitting gets really provocative is when it is applied to bodies. Certain bodies "fit" the shape of their environments, while other bodies do not. But here's the thing: Your body might fit a particular environment where mine misfits, but when the environment changes, our respective fitting and misfitting may also shift. In other words, my disabled blind body will be a misfit in a space where sight is required, but when we end up in the dark, my body will fit just fine. I can navigate without the benefit of vision; in the dark, your visually oriented body is the misfit. So fitting and misfitting are contextual; they are not stable states of existence. I fit here, you misfit there; you fit there, I misfit here.

Let's return to my four problematic parallels of the sinner, saint, and supercrip controlling images to explore what happens when we apply the theoretical concept of misfitting to them. Disability as misfit locates the "problem" or challenges of disability in the encounter between body and environment, not exclusively in the lack or failure of the individual body. The problem is not that the body does not "work"; rather, the problem is that the body does not work in the way that the environment expects it to function. In this way, finding accommodations for how to make the body and environment fit better becomes a structural issue that the community must reconcile, not just an issue of fixing the impaired individual body.

Disability as misfit erodes the us/them dichotomy. All bodies move in and out of fitting, depending on their specific environments. As environments shift, so do bodily fits. The notion of misfit reveals how everyone, disabled or not, is most likely at some point a misfit. As those of us with disabilities like to point out, if you live long enough, you will experience some form of physical limitation or disability. But even without physical limitations, many of us experience moments of misfitting due to race, sexual orientation, sexual identity, gender, or class; because our bodies don't conform to what society defines as thin; or simply because we are out of place in a particular situation. Thus, disability as misfit equalizes experiences of fitting and not fitting, of belonging and not belonging.

Disability as misfit moreover recasts the formula that disability equals suffering. It illuminates how, rather than being a natural state of suffering, disability is a challenging encounter between flesh and world, or a misfit. If we begin with the assertion that a body that does not fit a particular situation does not inherently have a bodily "problem" but rather is experiencing the failure of the environment to accommodate multiple fits and expressions of embodiment, suffering transforms into an opportunity for creative and collective problem-solving. We can explore and develop strategies to minimize the experiences of misfitting due to barriers to access, belonging, or participation. The true cause of suffering is residing outside the reach of human connection and community, not having a body with some limitations. Communities—religious or otherwise—can work together to ensure that fitting is the guidepost for all its members.

Disability as misfit erases the impulse of pity because it clarifies that while I am a misfit here, you are a misfit there. We all share in the experiences of fitting and misfitting. It is difficult to pity you as a misfit because I am also a misfit in some places and at some times. Genuine equality becomes possible if pity is removed from the equation. Replacing negative and ableist controlling images such as the sinner, saint, or supercrip with a positive controlling image like the misfit disrupts systems of power and privilege buttressing ableism.

Disability as misfit challenges ableism by allowing subjective knowledge and experience to produce oppositional consciousness and political identity. Misfits often occupy a vantage point that reveals where injustice and discrimination happen in the context of a community. If the community can listen to the voices of misfits, they can begin to work together to adjust the environment to establish the widest range of fits for the largest number of bodies. Misfitting reveals the reality that disability is just one form of human variation. It is precisely through the honest acknowledgment, celebration, and challenge of our variation that we create just communities, religious or otherwise.

What I really want to say to the airport assistants, acupuncturists, aunts, cousins, or anyone else who casts me as a faithless sinner, admirable saint, or heroic supercrip is that, in reality, I'm a badass misfit! But I also want to tell these same people that they, too, are badass misfits. I want them to realize that we are not that different. This is not to say that disability does not matter or that there are not challenges specific to living with a disability; rather, it is to say that misfitting is a way of being in the world that we all can embrace. Fitting and misfitting depend on the "dynamic encounter between flesh and world." I misfit in a busy airport because it's hard for me to get from gate to gate, but that's why I get help. I fit in my work environment because I fought hard to earn the requisite degrees and qualifications but also because I know my way around campus, and I easily move from building to building.

I want to invite the people I know and love to join me in some badass misfitting. I want to tell the strangers who appear to feel entitled to judge me that they should watch out and mind their own business because they are in the presence of a badass misfit! I want to invite religious communities to embrace misfitting while at the same time commit to expanding their range of fits.

~ 4 ~

Challenging Normalcy

"The body of Christ" and "The cup of salvation"—these phrases, or some variations thereof, are among the most commonly recited words in Christian worship services. If you're a Christian who comes from a Catholic, Episcopal, or Lutheran denomination, you probably hear them weekly; if you attend a church in most other Protestant denominations, you most likely hear them monthly or quarterly. These phrases frame the Christian ritual called Communion. Many Christians believe that Communion is a "sacrament," or an outward and visible sign of inward and invisible grace. Non-Christians often think of Communion as a weird, creepy, borderline cannibalistic practice where Christians pretend to eat the body and drink the blood of their God. For me, Communion is a fraught ritual, in both theological and practical terms.

I won't dive deep into my theological Communion conundrum here; that's a topic for another book. Rather, let me try to explain how and why the Episcopal Communion ritual troubles me in practical terms. Since my marriage, I have spent many a Sunday morning sitting in the pews of various Episcopal churches holding an internal debate about Communion. When I first started dating my now husband, Jonathan, I was a devoted nonchurchgoer. Growing up the dutiful daughter of a Mennonite minister where biweekly church attendance was the minimum, I figured I had already logged a lifetime of church attendance by the time I graduated from high school, and I needed a break from all things churchy. I returned to sporadic church attendance with Jonathan while in the flush of new love. In those first few years, I opted out of Communion because it felt disingenuous to participate in this holy sacrament when my relationship with Christian doctrine was ambivalent at best. I eventually came around to the thinking that the purpose of Communion was as much about being in community with other people as it was about confessing adherence to a particular set of beliefs, and so I felt less conflicted about participating in the ritual. By the time I worked my way around to taking Communion semiregularly, Jonathan was the priest celebrating the Eucharist. The simple shift from Jonathan sitting in the pews with me (as he did when we were first dating) to him standing at the altar distributing the bread is where things got complicated for me on a practical level.

The mechanics of the Christian ritual of Communion varies somewhat among denominations, but in most Episcopal contexts, it goes something like the following. The priest, or celebrant, as they are also called, recites the Eucharistic prayer during which, among other things, the priest blesses the bread and wine. Episcopalians, unlike Catholics, do not believe that the substances of bread and wine literally transform into the body and blood of Christ; rather, they believe that they are symbolic representations. So when Episcopalians (and other Protestants) receive the bread and wine, they believe that they are consuming bread and wine. (This may not entirely assuage the cannibalism concern for non-Christians, but it helps.) After the Eucharistic prayer, congregants typically file up to the altar to receive bread from the priest and wine from a chalice bearer, who distributes the wine. Sometimes people kneel at the altar, sometimes they remain standing. Then congregants return to their pews to sit quietly, sing, or pray while they wait for everyone to finish the trek to the Communion rail.

Sounds straightforward enough, right? Unless, of course, you are physically disabled. Suddenly, the weekly ritual, effortless for most able-bodied people, becomes entangled in complicated nego- tiations of space and motion. When Jonathan sits next to me in the pew, participating in Communion is as easy as grabbing his arm and walking up to the altar rail. But even then, I've experienced wine mishaps where the chalice bearer did not realize I was blind, and the cup ended up at nose or eye level instead of my mouth. I usually remedy these blunders easily enough and manage a sip of wine while sharing a quiet giggle with the chalice bearer. Sitting by myself presents more complications. Now I must figure out if I should attempt to get to the altar rail on my own with the help of my guide dog, stay seated and wait until the very end of the ritual for the priest and chalice bearer to come to me, accept the offer of a friendly parishioner to go up to the rail with them, or skip the whole thing and just opt out.

You might be thinking that this is a list of mostly great options for my Communion dilemma, but all these options reinforce ableism. Attempting to get to the altar rail with my guide dog puts me on disabled display—one of my absolute least favorite things about being blind. Almost without exception, my friends and family report that every time I move through the world with my guide dog, passers-by stare and ooh and ah. Both parts of this response piss me off. I do not want my disabled body and my mobility aid to be the object of your fascinated, curious stare, nor do I want you to respond to me with a tone typically reserved for babies, puppies, or other infantile creatures. Rosemarie Garland-Thomson writes about staring as a way of making sense of things we do not recognize or understand, or of the "strange or unfamiliar."[1] In my case, I suspect that people stare not so much because they think I am strange or unfamiliar but because they find the sight of a beautiful dog guiding someone through the world a remarkable thing. It is remarkable, and I understand the urge to stare or make obnoxious cooing sounds. But it's still ableist. It turns me into the "other," into an abnormal, unexpected, inexplicable focus of scrutiny, admiration, disgust, and so on. I do not appreciate being watched while I go about living my life.

The paradox here is that even as disabled bodies are the focus of so many stares, who we are and what we need go largely unseen. Garland-Thomson puts it well when she notes, "Indeed, the history of disabled people in the western world is in part the history of being on display, of being visually conspicuous while being politically and socially erased."[2] I long for the reverse: not being on display but being politically and socially relevant.

The next option—waiting for Communion to be delivered to me—shares some of the same problems as the first choice. Even if I do not trudge up to the rail with my dog, the whole congregation still focuses on me as the priest and chalice bearer parade to me (and other folks with mobility issues) with bread and wine in tow. Everyone watches as I receive Communion from my seat in the sanctuary. I imagine that they are thinking thoughts in that same baby tone that they use to address my dog about how sweet it is that the priest comes to me. I can't verify that other worshippers coo internally, but I most definitely feel the congregational gaze shift to me and the Communion entourage. Once again, I am on display. But what I find even more distressing about this mode of Communion distribution is that those of us who receive Communion from our pews are always served last. Being last is gross not only because you get the last drops of wine complete with everyone else's backwash but also because it makes me feel like an afterthought, like I get the last crumbs of bread, the last dregs of wine. Regardless of where I am physically sitting, I am located at the periphery of the Eucharistic community, at the end of the line of the faithful receiving the holiest of sacraments.

Perhaps the third option of going to the altar rail with another parishioner seems like the best option. It most closely mimics the easiest option, which is to go up with Jonathan. My comfort level with this choice, however, depends on how comfortable my sighted guide is with guiding. "Sighted guide" is the official term used for the people who assist a blind person in navigating through the world. What most folks don't know is that there are actual protocols for guiding a blind person, and believe me when I say that hardly anyone knows the "official" protocol! Most of my wonderfully well-meaning friends grab my arm and try to guide me by pulling or pushing me in the direction we need to go. When I first met Jonathan, due to his height (he is a solid nine inches taller than me), his preferred method of guiding me was to grab the back of my neck and steer me through public spaces. Writing this now makes it sound weirder than it felt at the time, but grabbing my arm or neck and pushing, pulling, or steering me does not fall into the category of proper protocol!

The correct way is for me to grab the arm of my sighted guide and walk about a half-step behind them. This method imitates what I do with my guide dog: I hold on to the dog's harness handle and walk a little behind the back of the harness, which allows me to follow the dog's lead as we wind our way through a crowd, restaurant, or any public place. Whether human or canine, if the guide veers left or right, I smoothly follow their lead. Even though the process seems counterintuitive to most of my sighted guides—I remind friends all the time that I grab them, not the reverse—it really is the nimblest way to do sighted guiding. If we hit a tight spot and need to walk single file, the sighted guide folds the arm I am holding behind their back, nonverbally cuing me to slip directly behind them. If we enter or exit a door, the sighted guide tells me that the hinge is on either the left or the right so that I know which side the door is on and how to maneuver through. These are simple details that, when carried out according to standard practice, enable me to move seamlessly through the world. What all of this means is that walking to the Communion rail with someone other than Jonathan can be either a smooth process or a bumbling mess, coupled with frenzied apologies, depending on the instincts and experience of my untrained sighted guide. It may not sound like a big deal, but honestly, it's usually just less stressful or complicated to decline the offer of assistance, stay seated, and skip Communion.

I hope that by this point in the book, it is obvious why the last choice—opting out of Communion altogether—is problematic and ableist. Anytime a person with a disability decides it is easier not to participate in a religious ritual or in any community activity than to expect the accommodations required for full inclusion and participation, that community has an ableism problem. And yet I make this choice all the time. Part of this is on me, but part of it is on society and the people around me. I get caught up in not wanting to be a "burden," a "pain," or "difficult." The handful of readers who have encountered me in real life are probably rolling their eyes right about now because I am not meek about my needs (or anything)! As my mother-in-law once said when she thought I was not listening, "Darla is good at getting her needs met!" I am indeed good at getting my needs met, but there is always an internal cost-benefit analysis involved. I always have to decide whether a given inaccessible situation is worth creating a fuss about. Check out the words I just used, "creating a fuss." Once again, internalized ableism rears its ugly head! Why should I equate insisting on full access and participation with "creating a fuss"? This is the part that's on me: I must reframe my thinking about asking for help. I must think of it not as creating a fuss but rather as requesting reasonable accommodations for access, inclusion, and participation.

But there is a second part, and this is the part that is on society and the people around me. I, or any person with a disability, should not always need to ask to be included or to be given access. Communities, religious or otherwise, should anticipate inclusion needs before people with disabilities need to ask. You should think about it before your disabled friends, family members, colleagues, schoolmates, or other community members need to ask. The tricky thing here is that every situation is different, and thus every situation requires different access solutions. A single solution rarely guarantees full participation and inclusion. Different disabilities require different accommodations, and ascertaining which adjustments will provide the most access for the greatest number of people with a wide variety of accommodation needs is challenging.

I could provide a long list of practical solutions for anticipating a variety of accessibility needs. But while that work is important, there is yet another layer we must peel back when considering access and accommodation issues, and it is one rarely tackled by religious or other communities. This is the layer underneath all the practical accommodation questions about how to include disabled bodies, the layer beyond the pew cuts for wheelchairs, the American Sign Language (ASL) interpreters, the braille service leaflets and hymnals, or the parade of Communion elements for those unable to get to the altar rail.

Sticking with my peeling layers metaphor, let's assume we are peeling back the layers of an onion. As you peel away the thin layers of onion skin, you eventually reach the firmer core of the onion. The core provides structure for the whole of the onion; without the core, the layers collapse into a pile of slimy onion skins. The question driving my onion metaphor is, What constitutes the core for how religious (and other) communities approach access, inclusion, and accommodation needs? In other words, what do we discover when we peel back the layers and reveal what lies at the core of how able-bodied people perceive disability? We discover that conceptions and definitions of normalcy hide beneath the layers. The core, in other words, is based on an intransigent understanding of what is normal.

Let's return to Ella, who we met in the previous chapter. Reflecting on growing up with a disability, Ella relayed a story about an interaction she had with her sixth-grade teacher at a Christian school: "I remember in sixth grade, I . . . at the time I was in a private Christian school, and something or other came up during morning devotion where my teacher asked me a question about whether I would want God to heal me or not. And I told her no. I said, 'This is the way God made me, like, I'm totally fine with this.'" Ella's teacher was "absolutely astounded" that Ella did not think of disability as a negative state of being. Six months later, the teacher still marveled at Ella's audacious attitude toward disability and brought it up again during a parent-teacher conference. She continued to be baffled that Ella was "totally fine" with her disabled body.

Ella's response to the question about healing exposed not only her teacher's assumptions about what it meant to have a "normal" body and live a "normal" life but also, and more significantly, repudiated the unquestioned cultural constructions of "normal" reflected through the teacher's befuddlement. "Even as a kid, it was always this thought: This is the way God made me. Like, sometimes it's not very fun, but, you know, I don't know anything different, like this is my normal." While Ella's thinking about disability became more sophisticated as she grew into adulthood, the innocent candor of her childhood response captures how many people living with disabilities feel about their nonnormative bodies: This is just my "normal." With profound simplicity, she expresses the driving force that underpins more complicated articulations of disability theory and activism.

The teacher's response to Ella's disability demonstrates a cultural truism, which is that we live in a society with narrow definitions of what it means to be "normal." Put another way, we live in a culture obsessed with the belief that there is such a thing as a "normal" body. Take a moment to reflect on how ideas of the norm permeate all arenas of culture and society. We measure intelligence using IQ tests, with scores falling above, below, or within the "normal" range. Young children make annual treks to the doctor to check their height and weight, during which parents learn if their child is growing at a "normal" rate. Conversations about everyday matters abound in all corners of domestic and professional life when people make comments like "That behavior is just not normal," "That is not a normal response," or "I just want to be normal." Whether referring to intelligence, physical attributes, or vague notions of social appropriateness, one thing is certain: We live in a culture propelled by what disability and literary theorist Lennard Davis calls the "hegemony of normalcy."[3]

The "hegemony of normalcy" means, first, that a commonly held definition of "normal" exists and, second, that "normal" is the ideal standard, the superior way to be, the most desirable. The parameters of normal can apply to any category of things, but for our purposes, I refer to what it means to inhabit a "normal" and "abnormal" body. I contemplate questions of normal and abnormal bodies with respect to disability, but of course the cultural definition of normal bodies extends well beyond physical or cognitive ability. The "normal" American body—in other words, the body against which all bodies are measured—is white, male, able-bodied, cisgender, strong, mentally stable, and so on. All bodies that do not fit these descriptors fall outside the range of normal.

When I was taking my first gender and women's studies class in college, we simply referred to the normal body as "Norman." We know what Norman looks like, but where did he come from? Or put another way: How did we end up with such stark distinctions between abnormal and normal bodies? What is the genesis of the concept of disability? Why does it matter if there is a standard for the normal body? What are the consequences of clinging to not only the idea but also the reality of Norman, especially with respect to disability?

Lennard Davis provides some helpful guidance for these questions when he argues that "disability" only became a cultural problem once a clear understanding of normalcy emerged. Davis notes that in ancient Greek societies, prior to any assertion of a "norm," the benchmark for human striving was the ideal of the gods. According to Davis, these societies understood human bodies as inferior imitations of the ideal bodily forms of the gods. An ideal, by definition, is unattainable, removing the expectation that any mere mortal could achieve it. Thus, all humans held a relatively equal inferior, nonideal, or one could say disabled status in comparison to the ideal of the gods.

Normalcy, Davis goes on to assert, emerged as a concept in the mid-nineteenth century when a confluence of scientific theories and ideologies merged to form our contemporary conception of the "norm" or "normal." First, the new field of statistics introduced methods for establishing and measuring "average" results. A second statistical innovation, the bell curve, offered experts a way to chart how individuals compare with the average. This system of hierarchical ranking not only asserted an average but also produced a category of statistical outliers from the average, or "norm."

Outliers fall above and below the average of the bell curve. Many people are happy to be categorized as outliers if they rank above the curve, such as in the case of the measure of intelligence. Most people, however, are not only satisfied to sit comfortably in the range of the average but strive for the normal ranking. We rarely, if ever, desire to be the outliers who rank below the curve. To fall below the curve is to be negatively outside the boundaries of the standard, the average, or the normal. Society extols bodies that outperform the average, but it disapproves of bodies that are ranked below the norm.

These ways of thinking about normalcy, when combined with the science of eugenics in the late nineteenth and early twentieth centuries, supplied a means for increasing the average and reducing deviance. Thus, the science of statistics established standard and nonstandard populations; the science of eugenics attempted to eradicate the nonstandard population.

And there it is. Once we established a system for developing standards or norms against which all else can be measured, it was not long before some began to believe that everything—or every body—that does not conform to the standard should be eliminated. This is the consequence of clinging to the concept of Norman: It moves quickly from believing that there is a normal way of being to having no tolerance for bodies that do not or cannot conform to the norm. The next step is to find ways to dispose of those bodies.

The association between eugenics and "normal" has far-reaching and devastating consequences for disabled bodies. We see these ideas propagated throughout culture, in novels, poetry, the phenomenon of the freak show, and visual and performance art. As I noted in chapter 1, religion is one of the most significant influences shaping culture. As such, religious texts, art, rituals, practices, and teachings are also important sites where cultures construct, establish, and assert their "norm." While it is unlikely that Ella's teacher consciously considered whether she was propagating the "hegemony of normalcy" or asked herself where her ideas about "normal" bodies originated, it is probably safe to assume that religion and religious teachings influenced the Christian teacher's astonishment about Ella's nonchalant attitude toward disability. Ella and her teacher had different definitions of "normal." A disabled body fit Ella's definition of normal, but for Ella's teacher, disability was most decidedly outside the range of normalcy.

Most of my other interviewees did not communicate their understanding of normalcy with Ella's sharp precision. What they were clear about, however, was that each of their respective religious communities made their expectations for "normal" bodies exceedingly clear, particularly when it came to participating in religious rituals. Their communities moreover made abundantly clear that anyone who was unable to participate fully in religious rituals in the prescribed way would remain on the periphery of the community or would be pushed out altogether.

As I note throughout this book, religious communities are not, for the most part, malicious in their excluding tendencies. They do not intentionally push people with disabilities to the margins or outside the bounds of their respective communities. I assure you that everyone at the Episcopal churches I have attended would be heartbroken to learn that I at times felt excluded from Communion. But this is exactly what I am asking you to think about: the insidious and ubiquitous nature of the hegemony of normalcy. We don't notice it because it is so ingrained in how we think, act, and believe—it is baked into our fundamental worldview. But whether malicious and intentional or not, the consequences are the same. The best-case scenario is that people with disabilities are excluded because they are not normal; in the worst-case scenario, people with disabilities are eliminated because they are not normal. Both options are unacceptable; both options are destructive; both options are ableist.

It is no longer acceptable to shrug off responsibility for perpetuating normalcy, which also perpetuates ableism, just because it is baked into your worldview. To rage against ableism is to consciously expose the ugly nature of Norman. We can expose

Norman's destructive power by mining sites of cultural production and unearthing the oppressive bedrock, including those based on religion.

It is, of course, impossible to excavate every way that religious communities construct and reinforce normalcy. Norms are not created in a single location or via a single process. Instead, I offer a few snapshots of how the forces producing and perpetuating Norman play out in religious communities and contexts. We could pick any number of examples to explore, but the few examples I use demonstrate as well as any how underlying systems and structures of inequity, exclusion, and marginalization function in religious communities by designating some bodies as "normal" and others as "abnormal." In this way, religious communities participate, most often unwittingly, in a form of the eugenic project: the erasure or elimination of the nonnormative body.

Art simultaneously reflects and creates societal standards and values. A survey of religious art can therefore teach us something about religious values and beliefs. The late disability theorist Tobin Seibers contended that art both reflects how humans see themselves and reveals the things they have tried to keep hidden.[4] What, then, do works of religious art reflect and reveal about how religious communities perceive the human body—especially the disabled body—and what do they try to conceal about those perceptions?

Images and representations of nonnormative or disabled bodies appear throughout the history of artistic representations, but until relatively recently, art historians have not paid much attention to the role of disability in works of art. As Ann Millett-Gallant and Elizabeth Howie note in their introduction to their book *Disability and Art History*, the scholarly discipline of art history was born in the nineteenth century, paralleling the period when the medical model of disability established its stronghold as the standard mode for interpreting disability. Perhaps it is not surprising, then, that when art historians did write about disability, they failed to consider how disability as a category is socially and culturally constructed. This is so much the case, Millett-Gallant and Howie marvel, that it is even difficult to find works of art or scholarly articles depicting disability through database queries using the term "disability." Rather, they note, "the researcher must use pejorative terms such as 'cripple' and 'lame,' or even more troubling, perhaps, 'fool' as well as other descriptive terms such as 'blind,' in order to find art historical analysis of such works."[5]

The scholarship about the early Dutch Renaissance artist Hieronymus Bosch, for example, exhibits the phenomenon, so troubling to Millett-Gallant and Howie, that conflates disability with pejorative terms and descriptors. In an attempt to elicit Christian compassion among his viewers, Bosch included deformed figures, such as "crippled" beggars, in his paintings. Erwin Pokorny argues, however, that instead of eliciting compassion, Bosch's contemporaries would have responded to these representations of crippled beggars with feelings of fear and disdain: fear of poverty and disease and disdain for those whose bodies they believed bore the marks of sin and God's subsequent punishment. The normative body was a virtuous body, free from apparent and hidden maladies. Conversely, crippled, impoverished, or disabled bodies signified moral and spiritual failure. Bosch's representations of crippled beggars often resembled deformed devils, cementing the link between disability and evil or sin.[6]

The example of Bosch's crippled beggars illuminates how visual representations create and reproduce a bodily norm, which in turn creates and reproduces the abnormal or the other. Religious art, especially, holds symbolic power because it implies that the bodily norm reflects God's favor—or the lack thereof. In other words, a healthy body corresponds with virtue, which in turn equals assurances of salvation. A deformed or disabled body, in contrast, reveals immorality, which subsequently excludes one from salvific reassurances. Religious art, including Bosch's paintings, reinforces the idea that the body exposes virtuousness and nonvirtuousness.

When combined with the belief that disability can be healed by faith, disability in religious art becomes a glaring sign that an individual is spiritually depraved, abnormal, and "other."

I spent a lot of time in chapter 3 exploring where controlling images of people with disabilities originate. In that chapter, I focused on Christian gospel accounts of Jesus's interactions with disabled people to draw a connection to the sinner controlling image, but Bosch's art is yet another example of how sin gets equated with disability. In the case of Bosch's art, the story burns into the collective imaginary through visual imagery, which is equally if not more powerful than stories told through words for those in the sighted world.

I recently traveled to Québec City for a quick romantic getaway with Jonathan. The architectural and strategic ingenuity of the sixteenth-century French colonizers who constructed a walled city on a cliff overlooking one of the narrowest parts of the St. Lawrence Seaway, ensuring their military advantage against invaders, amazed me. The incredible food blew me away—I had one of the best dining experiences of my life that week. The European feel of Québec City surprised me, even though many friends and relatives had told me what to expect. The history, food, culture, and people of Québec City fascinated me, but a quiet moment in the basilica of Sainte-Anne-de-Beaupré on the Île d'Orléans, about three miles outside the old part of Québec City, left the most lasting impression.

One of the eight national shrines of Canada, Saint Anne attracts almost a million pilgrims each year. The Catholic Church asserts that many miracles of curing the sick and disabled occur at the basilica, hence many of the pilgrims who journey to Saint Anne arrive seeking healing.

As Jonathan and I walked up to the grand structure, I joked that maybe Saint Anne would cure me. As I expected, she did not! But what I had not expected was the range of strong emotions I felt when I entered the church and stood by the hundreds of discarded crutches, canes, and other disability-related aides left by pilgrims who apparently found the cure they sought. I felt cynical about

FIG. 1. Column displaying discarded crutches and canes at Sainte-Anne-de-Beaupré Basilica near Québec City (iStock)

how these people were duped into believing that they were cured, and I wondered what would happen when they got home and their ailments reared up again. I felt curious about whether I was wrong, and I wondered if those people really were cured because they believed something that I could not. I felt maybe just a little jealous that I did not possess that kind of faith and therefore could not even be open to the possibility of miraculous healing.

But mostly, I felt an overwhelming sense of sadness and anger that the thousands of disabled pilgrims who sojourned to Saint Anne over the centuries believed, truly believed, that their disability was somehow inextricably linked to how much they believed, to how much faith they did or did not have. I felt sad and angry that in the presence of their God, in the midst of their church and community, these disabled pilgrims did not believe that their disabled bodies were enough. They did not have faith that they were as worthy and valuable as people who appeared to have able bodies. I felt sad and angry that disabled pilgrims longed to be normal, which meant no longer disabled. For most of the visitors to the sacred space of the Basilica of Sainte-Anne-de-Beaupré, the discarded signs of disability symbolized great faith and the power of the divine. For me, they symbolized the erasure and elimination of disabled bodies. They told me that my disabled body was unholy, immoral, and unvirtuous. In that holy space, I felt like one of Bosch's deformed devils.

I thought about Bosch's deformed devils at Saint Anne's shrine because I was doing research for this book, but most pilgrims almost certainly are not making these connections. We might reasonably ask, How much do the perceptions revealed and reflected through religious art influence how people in subsequent times think about disability? Here, it is useful to remember that the culture gets its power not just from how people receive it in the moment they consume it but by establishing broader social and cultural norms. Effective cultural productions, whether works of art or novels, are infused into the cultural imagination and subsequently are passed on from one generation to the next.

Ella's teacher most likely never saw a Bosch painting. Even if she had, she most likely would not have drawn a direct line between what she saw in the painting and what she thought about disability. But the point here is not whether Ella's teacher or the millions of pilgrims who trek to Saint Anne had personally seen Bosch's deformed devils; the point is that forms of cultural production influence how we think about other people. They shape our prejudices without our conscious awareness. Once those prejudices are lodged in our imagination, we construct community rituals, practices, standards, and so on based on those prejudices.

Even though religious art is just one form of cultural production, we can detect echoes of Bosch's deformed devils in other moments of religious history and communities. The writings and teachings of colonial-era American minister and self-appointed medical adviser Cotton Mather, for instance, show how the ghosts of earlier representations of normativity haunt later historical periods. Church historian and reverend Heather Vacek notes that Cotton Mather was born into one of the most prominent families of late seventeenth- and early eighteenth-century colonial America. Vacek observes that Mather combined a unique blend of theological and medical instruction into his preaching, writing, and advising.[7]

Vacek goes on to assert that Mather fervently believed that the primary explanation for the cause of sickness was sin: "Bear in mind that sin was that which first brought sickness upon a sinful world, and which yet continues to sicken the world, with a world of diseases."[8] For Mather, two forms of sin answered the age-old question of how evil could persist in a world created by a good and all-powerful God: original and individual sin. Mather cited the example of innocent yet deformed or diseased infants as "proof" of original sin: "This wretched [diseased or deformed] infant has not arrived upon years of sense enough, to sin after the similitude of the transgression committed by Adam. Nevertheless, the transgression of Adam . . . has involved this infant in the guilt of it."[9] Although sick infants bore no responsibility for their "wretched" plights, Mather insisted that through acts of individual sin, sick or disabled adults shouldered the blame for their maladies.

Mather grounded his theorizing about the linkages between sin and disease or disability in the Christian Bible. Psalm 107:17 was one of many passages Mather invoked as evidence for his theological proclamation that individual sin explained illness and disability: "Fools, because of their transgression, and because of their iniquities are afflicted, with sickness."[10] For Mather, as well as for the majority of his Puritan followers, diseased and disabled bodies were pitiable, reprehensible indications of a sinful soul. Mather even went as far as to invoke the devil or satanic possession as a plausible explanation for mental illness or melancholy.

Note how both Bosch and Mather invoke the devil when referring to (in Mather's case) or depicting (in Bosch's case) disease and disability. Bosch's deformed devils provide a window into how works of religious art symbolically create and reinforce the universality of the normal body. Mather's references to the devil attest to the ways cultural assumptions about normativity seep into religious preaching and writing. I cannot draw a direct line from Bosch to Mather. Yet parallels exist between what Bosch silently conveys through his paintings and what Mather loudly proclaims through his preaching and writing about sick, diseased, and disabled bodies. In each case, disabled bodies indicate sin and immorality; in each case, healthy bodies epitomize virtue and divine favor.

The vast majority of my interviewees reported encountering people in their religious communities who also, implicitly or explicitly, drew connections between sin and disability. Does this mean that these people saw Bosch's paintings or read Mather's corpus? Most likely not, but they would have no need. A multitude of cultural texts, including but not limited to paintings, novels, poems, biblical passages, movies, photographs, sermons—the list goes on and on—assert the same message about nonnormative bodies. As messages about normalcy seep into the cultural imagination, they trickle down and through generations. Eventually, and often quickly, these messages settle into the broader culture and then morph into unquestioned truisms.

*   *   *

Take a moment to consider representations of disability and people with disabilities you have encountered in some of the cultural texts I previously mentioned. If you belong to a religious community, do the same thought exercise for your sacred texts, religious rituals, and public teachings or sermons. Where and how does the hegemony of normalcy show up? How are bodies—disabled or not—represented? What implicit or explicit connections do these texts draw between bodies and other images, ideas, or metaphors? Who is and is not included in these cultural texts? How are nonnormative bodies portrayed? Why are these questions important?

My interviewees encountered a variety of attitudes about the normality/abnormality of disabled bodies in their respective religious communities. Some of their stories revealed blatant attitudes equating sin and disability, but more common were stories that recounted more subtle messages. One blind minister described how the ordaining board of his denomination initially declined to ordain him because they were concerned that a blind person could not fulfill all the responsibilities of ministry. He had already completed the required degrees, trainings, and experiences, but because he was disabled, he was denied ordination. No one on the committee explicitly stated that his body did not fit their standards of embodied normalcy. Rather, they shrouded their attitudes about normalcy in questions about how he would read the gospel or how he would visit shut-ins, given that he could not drive. These are reasonable questions to problem-solve, but they are not grounds for denial of a call to ministry. The story has a happy ending because another configuration of the ordination board eventually approved him.

We can celebrate a happy ending—it's a great resolution. But a happy ending often allows us to dismiss the obstacles a person encountered along the way. This man was not ultimately ordained because the standards of embodied normalcy suddenly changed; he was ordained because he persevered and luckily ended up with a more enlightened ordination board.[11] The fact remains that another candidate with the same qualifications most likely would have breezed through the initial ordination process, with or without an enlightened committee.

Ideas about normalcy show up in all kinds of attitudes. When these attitudes relate to bodies, we must name them for what they are: ableist. Ableist attitudes in and of themselves are damaging, but they can also translate into discriminatory, exclusionary, or unjust practices. At best, ableist thinking in religious communities can result in exclusionary charity, where communities tolerate people with disabilities as pitiable presences but never include them as full participants in the life of the community. At worst, religious communities openly embrace ableist attitudes, leaving no room for people with disabilities and even sometimes fueling the belief that people with disabilities are unvirtuous, deformed devils. In either case, ableist religious communities deny people with disabilities full access to sacred space, community, and practice. When these beliefs shade into equating disability with immorality, ableist attitudes supply the rationale for eliminating disabled bodies altogether.

We are all aware of the horrors of what happens when exclusion slides into elimination. This is eugenics. I do not use this term lightly. Eugenics is the intentional, systematic elimination of individuals and entire groups of people deemed undesirable because of their perceived nonnormativity. Eugenics leads to the literal elimination of people, as in the Holocaust, but it also includes practices designed to control and shape reproduction, such as forced sterilization of disabled people and planned breeding. These forms of eugenics are immoral, indefensible acts.

I know I am wandering into tricky territory here, but I want us to think carefully about more subtle forms of eugenics, or what I refer to as "social eugenics." Social eugenics are practices that, by their design, exclude or eliminate people that any given community considers abnormal. In our case, "abnormal" refers to disabled people, but of course, it can refer to any minority identity. People of color, LGBTQ+ folks, immigrants, and other marginalized groups regularly experience the cascading consequences of social eugenics. Whether done intentionally or unintentionally, social eugenics creates homogeneous communities that expect the majority of bodies to look and function in a prescribed, "normal" fashion. In using the phrase "social eugenics," I want us to confront the reality that ableist attitudes, coupled with ableist practices, can eliminate people from our communities.

Religious ritual practices, with their blithe assumption of able bodies in motion, subtly yet powerfully communicate a community's bodily norms and standards. From the Islamic mandate to pray five times a day prostrating on a floor mat oriented toward Mecca; to the multiple forms of Buddhist meditation requiring practitioners to sit for many minutes or hours; to the Jewish rabbinical sacred duty of reading directly from the Torah scroll; to the many forms of Christian worship that involve standing, sitting, kneeling, or walking to and from the altar rail: religious ritual performance can simultaneously resemble a rigorous physical workout that excludes people with disabilities from the heart of communal ritual practices.

It may seem obvious to point out that it is difficult, at best, for people with physical disabilities to participate in these types of religious rituals. Take a moment to recall a time when you attended a house of worship where people with apparent disabilities were also in attendance. Were people with disabilities able to participate fully in all of the religious rituals, or did they observe from the sidelines? If you have not attended a religious service with people with disabilities, ask yourself if someone with a mobility, hearing, or cognitive disability could easily take part in the religious rituals in which you have participated.

Rituals matter because they define the terms and boundaries of community membership. Think about groups—religious or otherwise—in which you participate. It might be an educational setting, a civic organization, or a sports team. What are the "rituals" unique to that group? What are the signs that indicate to a new person who is an insider and who is an outsider?

Religious rituals in almost all religious contexts also simultaneously reflect, generate, perpetuate, and challenge community values and priorities. Whether formal or informal, religious rituals are scripted performances signaling what a community believes and values. Thus, religious rituals both convey who belongs in the group and communicate the values and beliefs of the group. Religious ritual performances, through their pre-scripted physical gestures and movements, also distinguish between normative and nonnormative bodies. For people with and without disabilities, the underlying assumption that a body must appear and function in a certain way to participate in ritual performance impedes the possibility of genuine inclusive, equitable, and justice-oriented communities. And because practitioners presume that religious ritual performances are sanctioned by and imbued with sacred, holy, and divine authority, they wield even more persuasive cultural power than most cultural texts.

My Communion dilemma illustrates how religious rituals designed for "normal" or able bodies fuel social eugenics. Recall how my options for participating in Communion reinforced ableism and in the most extreme case excluded me from the ritual. Christians describe the ritual of Communion as a sacred or holy meal. It is akin to a celebratory holiday meal where friends and family gather around a table to share food and create community. Imagine that your family sits down to Thanksgiving dinner, and you all turn to stare as one family member with a disability awkwardly approaches the table on their own. Or imagine that your disabled relative can't get to the table, so they sit alone in the living room while the rest of the family eats, and then they are served their meal after everyone else has finished. Or imagine that the person with a disability decides not to attend the family dinner because it is easier and more comfortable to stay at home and because they do not want to be a burden. These unthinkable options are how I frequently experience Christian Communion. My place either on the periphery of or entirely outside of the circles of the defining Christian ritual is a large part of why I stopped going to church. It's not the only reason, but it remains a significant factor.

The hegemony of embodied normalcy creates standards for how bodies should participate in a given community's rituals. Once standards exist, they determine who is and is not "normal." When religious communities center on ritual practices that exclude or eliminate abnormal bodies, they are practicing social eugenics. How can religious (and other) communities ensure that all members belong at the table?

One way that religious communities can begin to ensure that all bodies are welcome is to adapt religious rituals, practices, and bodily norms to include a wider range of embodied experiences. Disabled bodies disrupt the prescribed order of things when they do not—nay, cannot—conform to the normative bodily requirements for enacting religious ritual performances or for participating in the life of the community. But what happens to the ritual performance—and even more importantly to the life of the community—when disabled bodies insist on being full and equal actors in the performance of religious ritual? As theater scholar Jill Dolan submits, live performances, which for our purposes include live religious ritual performances, create space for "embodying and enacting new communities" by "actualizing" otherwise empty language on diversity.[12] Embodying, enacting, and creating new communities through inclusive religious ritual performances powerfully conveys that a religious community prioritizes access, inclusion, and justice.

Disability activist and scholar Shayda Kafai writes about disability performance art. She argues that "it creates a rebellious climate that elevates the performance of disability as an identity to the realm of protest, to where the body can 'cause commotion' and rewrite stigma."[13] Disabled bodies cause commotion through their mere presence in religious communities. Causing commotion is yet another form of raging against ableism because it insists on access, inclusion, and justice.

Mary, a Protestant minister who lives with rheumatoid arthritis and a disintegrating spine, illustrated the difference between religious communities that unconsciously assert an able-bodied norm and those that don't. Mary had served multiple churches at the time of our interview. The first congregation she talked about expected her to perform some rituals in the chancel. A chancel is typically where the choir sits and where the minister frequently presides over Communion or other rituals. In this particular church (as in most architecturally traditional church buildings), the chancel sits several steps up from the nave (the main part of the worship space). Mary's diagnoses affect her mobility, but her ease of mobility comes and goes, depending on unpredictable factors. Some days it was easy for her to walk up the steps to the chancel, but many other days it was not.

After struggling with the steps more often than not, Mary caused a commotion. "Look," Mary said to the congregation, "I'm not entering the chancel until there's a ramp or some accommodation is made. I just refuse." The congregation added a ramp. I responded to Mary's story by saying, "Wow, good for them." "Well," Mary retorted, "it was sad that it took that to get it done."

Having learned a valuable lesson through her experience with the chancel, Mary was upfront about her abilities and limitations with the search committee the next time she interviewed for a job. "I can't be picking up Bibles and moving chairs," Mary stated. The reply shocked her: "You don't have to do that here; we already plan for someone else to take care of that." In this case, Mary did not need to cause commotion because the community already anticipated and addressed access and inclusion needs.

I long for the day when Mary and I—and all people with disabilities—no longer need to cause commotion to participate fully in the ritual life of a religious community. I long for the day when this body that I inhabit is counted as just another normal body. Or, better yet, when categories of normal and abnormal bodies no longer hold relevance or power within religious communities.

I have participated in religious services with people with intellectual and developmental disabilities whose religious exuberance bursts through the formal rituals with spontaneous singing, hand-raising, or speaking. I have also witnessed the uncomfortable silence and covert glances as a person with a mobility disability moves through religious spaces slowly or with jerking, halting motions. Moments like these "cause commotion" for able-bodied participants, even if no motion occurs.

I cause commotion when I participate in Communion. I am not always willing to make this commotion, but I also know that my obvious presence and participation in religious ritual not only help me feel like a full member of the community but also move the entire community closer to disability justice.

When people with disabilities cause commotion, either intentionally or simply by virtue of existing in a space, they engage in a political act of justice making that insists that those usually relegated to the margins of a community are seen, heard, valued, and included. Commotion can be blatant or subtle, bold or discrete; either way, it refutes the ways many religious rituals reinforce the primacy of the normal body. But here's the thing: Causing commotion cannot just be the responsibility or priority of people with disabilities or other marginalized members of a community. The entire religious community must commit to causing commotion. Causing commotion surfaces as one powerful strategy for religious (and other) communities committed to dismantling the divisions of "normal" and "abnormal" and to reorienting the boundaries of inclusion.

~ 5 ~

Crip Tests

Have you encountered the theory that everyone can be divided into one of two types of binaries: dogs or cats, wine or beer, summer or winter, Pepsi or Coke, and so on? The genesis of the theory remains a mystery to me, but it makes for a fun icebreaker at a party if conversation lags. The most intense debates often revolve around dogs or cats: Rarely do people find a middle ground with this one. As for me, dogs all the way—also, wine, winter, and I hate both Pepsi and Coke!

As a well-trained academic, I try to avoid simple binaries like these examples (with the exception of dogs or cats because, seriously, cats?). I must confess, however, that I silently divide my friends and colleagues into two groups: people comfortable with my disability and people not comfortable with my disability. Most authors feel at least a twinge of nervousness about people reading their work. When I think about strangers or friends reading this book, I fly from zero to one hundred on the panic scale. Writing anything for public consumption makes me feel exposed and vulnerable. You might be surprised, though, to learn that I feel most nervous about my friends, family, and colleagues' reactions to this book, particularly the next several paragraphs. Why? First, everyone reading this who knows me likely thinks that they fall into the category of people who are comfortable with my disability. Second, everyone reading this who knows me is starting to get worried that I might not share their assessment of their comfort level with my disability. And here I've got bad news: You're right. You are not as comfortable with disability as you like to think you are.

While chugging along on the honesty train, I might as well also confess that I dread the postpublication conversations I will inevitably have with worried friends seeking reassurance that they fall into the "people who are comfortable with disability" group. And even if you don't know me personally, you should know that all of this still probably applies to you if you know anyone with a disability but are not yourself disabled.

My ability to tell the difference between people who are and are not comfortable with disability is difficult to put into words. The differences are often subtle and hard to pinpoint. For instance, I do not gauge a person's comfort with disability based on whether someone occasionally makes an unintentionally ableist comment. We all occasionally make unintentionally ableist, sexist, or racist comments because we live in a society where these -isms are so ingrained in our psyches that offensive words and metaphors sometimes slip out. I hear people using "blind" metaphors almost every day. I'm not suggesting that this excuses the comments or that we can't help ourselves. As I said in chapter 2, we all need to be ever mindful of the words we use, and we all need to make intentional efforts to do better. Nevertheless, ableist comments alone do not establish which side of the disability comfort dividing line a person is on.

Nor is the dividing line established by your skill at being my sighted guide. In fact, some of my friends who are most comfortable with my disability bang me into things all the time. If I had a dollar for every time a beloved friend crashed me into something, forgot to tell me about a step or curb, or forgot that I needed to grab their arm and walked away, leaving me stranded, I would be a wealthy woman! The banging, crashing, forgetting, or stranding does not determine comfort or discomfort with disability in and of itself. Rather—and here's the part that's hard to explain—it's the response to the banging, crashing, forgetting, and stranding that indicates how comfortable you are or are not with my disability.

I frequently use my friends as sighted guides, especially when I travel to larger cities for conferences. Toby, my current guide dog, is an excellent guide, but because he depends on me for instruction and direction, he is less helpful when we are in unfamiliar places where I don't know my way around. I often leave Toby at home if I'm attending a conference for only a few days. At one of these conferences, I was depending on my friend Jane as my sighted guide. As Jane and I marched down the sidewalk toward the session we planned to attend, deep in conversation, I unknowingly veered toward the curb, stepped crooked, and fell. I was wearing my standard conference uniform—a skirt and tights—and the fall ripped my tights and banged up my knee. I was not seriously hurt, but there was blood and a big hole in my tights. For the record: I fall or bang into things all the time. As my husband explained to one of his friends, "It's just a regular part of being blind." So on this day with Jane, I did what I normally do when I am not seriously hurt: I stood up and brushed myself off. I started calculating whether I had enough time to dash back to the hotel, clean up my knee, change my tights, and get to the session in time or whether I should continue to the session in my present state.

Jane, on the other hand, started melting down. "Oh my god," she exclaimed, "I am such an idiot. This is all my fault. I am such a bad friend. I am a terrible guide. People must think I am a horrible friend." Eventually, once her self-recriminating soliloquy ended, Jane remembered me and shifted the focus of her semihysterical ramble: "Oh shit, are you OK? You're bleeding; I ruined your tights; I'm so sorry; oh, crap, I'm such a bad friend."

I understand Jane's distressed response. It is distressing to feel responsible for a friend's mishap, even if totally accidental. But

Jane's response focused on Jane's feelings, especially how my fall reflected poorly on her. Instead of helping me figure out the best course of action, Jane spiraled. I was bleeding, wearing ripped tights, and trying to determine whether we could make it to the session in time, yet in the moment I felt like I needed to manage Jane's feelings of embarrassment and shame, even though I was the one who fell and was hurt. "I'm OK," I said in a slightly clipped tone. "It's not your fault. I fall all the time. Don't worry about it. I wasn't paying attention either."

The critical piece here is that I felt like I needed to manage Jane's feelings. This is what I mean when I say that your comfort with my disability is often revealed through your response to my banging, falling, crashing, or any multitude of situations where my disability is on full display. If I need to make you feel OK or comfortable or reassure you about my mishap, all of which are ways for you to ask me to make you feel more comfortable with my blindness, you probably are not as comfortable with disability as you think.

My example with Jane focuses on a mishap, but the same idea applies to responses to any disability-related situation or blunder. Shit happens because I am blind. I accidentally drop or push food off my plate. I direct a comment to a person in a meeting who, unbeknown to me, has quietly slipped out of the room. I ask a weird question because I misidentify someone's voice and think I am talking to a different person. I get disoriented on my small campus because I don't pay full attention and Toby wanders in the wrong direction. These and many other examples define the reality of my disabled life. The good news is that I am quite comfortable with my disabled reality. Your response in these moments gives me a window into how comfortable you are with my disabled reality.

Soon after I first met my friend Martha, she invited me out for coffee. We chatted about life details for a few minutes, and then Martha whipped out her notebook and said, "I know I'm going to say and do the wrong thing with respect to your disability, but I want you to tell me what is and is not helpful to you. What is the best way for me to assist you? What do people do that feels annoying and condescending?" No new friend had ever asked me these questions (especially the last one). Martha scribbled notes to all my answers. No one had ever taken notes about the best way to help me.

Months after our coffee outing, Martha and I attended a conference with our friend Kim, where I delivered one of the keynote addresses. As the three of us piled into an Uber to go to the conference venue on the morning of my talk, Martha accidentally slammed the door on my fingers. I shrieked, Martha shrieked, and then she opened the door, shouted an apology, and ran back into the hotel to grab a bag of ice. Let me be clear, Martha, like Jane, felt horrible. But unlike Jane, Martha did not need me to manage her feelings. She apologized and then got on with the business of doing what needed to be done.

I do not expect, or even need, all of my friends to take me out for coffee and take notes about disability. Many of my friends are perfectly comfortable with my blindness without the coffee date. Martha most likely did not "need" the coffee date to be comfortable with disability, but it was still a lovely gesture. My point here is that, when I break my own rule about binary thinking and divide my friends into categories of comfort and discomfort with disability, I base that judgment on two fundamental things: how you respond to my disability (including but not limited to moments of mishap) and what you need from me in relation to your response. If I expend a lot of energy managing your feelings or awkwardness about my blindness, you land in the "discomfort with disability" category.

True confessions: I play the same mental game with educational, religious, professional, or civic institutions and organizations with which I affiliate. Before plunging into researching and writing this book, I did not have the language or framework for explaining how I knew the difference between institutions that were or were not comfortable with disability. I could tell you which institutions were welcoming, inclusive, and accessible communities, but I might have struggled to explain how I knew this.

Through my interviews, I discovered that other people with disabilities also lacked the language to explain why they felt like they belonged in some religious spaces but not in others. The reasons behind these feelings are, of course, complicated, but part of the explanation comes from a religious community's collective comfort or discomfort with disability. As with individuals, communities respond to disability in distinct ways that reveal their comfort level with disability. If a community needs people with disabilities to manage the community's response to discomfort, I place them squarely in the "discomfort with disability" category. For institutions and communities, I also add a third litmus test that does not apply to individuals, which is to ask, When people with disabilities join a religious community, are they welcomed into the fold because the community genuinely values inclusion and diversity or because the presence of disabled members makes the community appear as though they embrace these commitments? In other words, does the presence of people with disabilities merely check the diversity and inclusion box? If our presence simply checks the box, the community most likely is not comfortable with disability.

Consider a cartoon that was once described to me showing a person in a wheelchair looking up at a flight of stairs leading into a house of worship brandishing a sign that proudly proclaims, "All Are Welcome." The message on the sign checks the box, but the absence of a ramp or an accessible entrance sends a different message. It is impossible to know which message is accurate without knowing more about a particular community, but a cursory analysis of the cartoon indicates that in this case, the community wants to appear inclusive, but it has yet to do the work to make it a reality.

The tricky thing here is that physical or architectural modifications alone do not necessarily answer the litmus test. Like the sign in the cartoon suggests, some communities say they are welcoming, but they really are not. Many other communities appear unwelcoming on the surface, but a closer examination tells a different story. I spent a delightful hour and a half on the phone interviewing Jonah—a Jewish man in his late thirties with CP. With limited dexterity in one hand, none in the other, and no use of his legs, Jonah uses a motorized wheelchair and a personal care assistant for mobility, getting dressed and undressed, and preparing food. Through advances in technology and what he called "training," Jonah requires less assistance for daily care needs as an adult than he did when he was younger. As Jonah explained to me, people who can manage their own urine only need help every ten or twelve hours as opposed to every one or two hours. Jonah moreover observed that, as he grows older, he is less afraid to ask for help. Asking for help, Jonah asserted, is simultaneously one of the most important and hardest skills for young people with disabilities to learn.

Jonah described his parents as Jewish professionals. His father was a rabbi in the Reform tradition, and his mother was an educator in the Conservative movement:

> Needless to say, my house was a very Jewish home, since it
> was not only the religion and practice of both parents but the
> profession of both parents. So it was sort of a live, breathe, eat,
> sleep kind of thing. We kept kosher, we had Shabbat rituals
> that were, you know, consistent for Reformed Judaism, but, you
> know, definitely a type of Shabbas [i.e., Sabbath] where we didn't
> do anything that, you know, we would have classified as work,
> although I wouldn't learn the thirty-nine categories of Halakah
> [laws of Jewish life] as an Orthodox conception of Shabbat until
> my formal education years later, because that would have had no
> bearing on my family's practice.

Jonah reported that he was active in his father's synagogue while growing up. He described his Jewish education as standard, celebrating his bar mitzvah at the traditional age of thirteen.

Jonah recalled that, for many years, he was the only person with an apparent disability at his synagogue and in the other religious

spaces he frequented. Jonah was carried in and out of the synagogue throughout his childhood because it only had stair access.
Jonah mused that no one made a big deal out of the fact that he
needed to be carried; it was just the reality. Whichever men were
available just carried him up and down the stairs. Jonah encountered a similar situation at the summer camp that he and his four
siblings attended while his parents worked as staff. There were no
ramps or other wheelchair accessibility features at the camp: "It
was just natural that when I reached camper age, [I would attend
camp,] though the camp had never before, you know, addressed
the questions of disability, being the mid-'80s. It was simply taken
as a given that they would figure out how I would participate, and
they did."

Jonah's childhood and adolescent religious communities always
found ways to include him, and he expressed gratitude for that.
There was never a question of whether he would be included;
rather, the question was always how. Even so, Jonah, who at the
time of our interview was a disability educator and inclusion
advocate, notes that these religious communities began to address
participation and access issues only when confronted with an individual with a disability.

As Jonah matured and his career developed, he became interested in the strategies of universal design. According to Ron Mace,
an architect with polio, who introduced the concept in the mid-
1980s, universal design (UD) is "design that's usable by all people,
to the greatest extent possible, without the need for adaptation
or specialized design."[1] Neither Jonah's synagogue nor the summer camp had implemented UD. If they had, those spaces would
have been accessible long before Jonah or anyone with a disability
arrived, eliminating the need for their on-the-spot problem-
solving. Many people with disabilities note that one of the most
misunderstood aspects of UD is that many individuals and communities believe that UD only applies to people with disabilities.
The reality is that, when a space is designed to accommodate the
needs of the disabled, it becomes more accessible for everyone. For
example, a building with a wheelchair ramp is accessible not just

for people who use wheelchairs but also for the elderly, parents with strollers, or someone temporarily using crutches.

In the middle of completing a law degree, practicing law, working for the National Council on Disability, and consulting with Jewish communities about implementing UD, Jonah applied to and was accepted to rabbinical school. In a somewhat ironic twist, however, Jonah was not able to attend because the institution was unable to provide the disability accommodations Jonah requires. In a teasing tone, Jonah laughed and said, "We'll see if I'm still interested when they figure it out. It's a work in progress."

Jonah's story reminds us that people with disabilities can never assume that access is guaranteed nor that a respective community is comfortable with disability in its midst. As Jonah's early experiences indicate, sometimes religious communities are comfortable with disability and find ways to seamlessly include disabled bodies into their practice, even when architectural barriers exist. More often, however, as Jonah discovered when the rabbinical school refused to accommodate him, religious communities are not comfortable with disabilities and impose structural barriers to people with disabilities. Jonah's story also reminds us that rarely does a community proactively address inclusion and access until confronted with a disabled body seeking access.

What is perhaps most infuriating is that people with disabilities can never predict which of the previous scenarios will greet them if they are bold enough to attempt to enter religious spaces. What is almost always true is that religious communities predictably treat disabled bodies as an identity that must be distinguished from the able-bodied status quo.

I think and read a lot about why and how institutions regulate which bodies fit into the status quo and which bodies do not. Over the course of my reading and thinking, I have developed a framework for making sense of how the process of regulating bodies, especially disabled bodies, happens in religious communities. I call this framework "crip tests." Crip tests are the ways in which able-bodied people in religious communities regulate and control if and how disabled persons are integrated into the community, thereby maintaining able-bodiedness as the dominant mode of embodiment, or what can be referred to as a nonidentity.

Here's the complicated thing about talking or writing about crip tests: Most if not all of the time, religious communities do not even realize they are deploying crip tests. The ways that religious (and other) communities regulate and control the participation of people with disabilities are so baked into taken-for-granted systems, structures, practices, rituals, beliefs, and so on that these processes remain largely hidden, even from the folks enacting them. By naming and describing the processes of crip tests, I hope to expose what happens beneath the surface in many religious communities.

Before launching into a description of how crip tests operate in religious communities, I want to highlight a couple of the more theoretical elements underlying how I think about crip tests. I am neither the first nor the only person to contemplate questions about how dominant groups regulate—intentionally or unintentionally—marginalized identities. For example, in his groundbreaking book *Crip Theory: Cultural Signs of Queerness and Disability*, Robert McRuer builds on lesbian feminist poet and theorist Adrienne Rich's understanding of compulsory heterosexuality.[2] McRuer argues that social actors cement compulsory able-bodiedness into the cultural imagination as unquestioned "normal" ways of existing in the world in the same way that they treat heterosexuality as an unquestioned normal. The important piece to understand is that when an identity is the unquestioned norm or so taken for granted that it becomes the standard identity, it becomes a nonidentity. We only notice identities that are set apart from, do not conform to, or stick out as different from the nonidentities we expect to encounter. One way to grasp how nonidentities work is to ask, How many people do you know who have intentionally come out as straight or able-bodied? Nonidentities are nonissues because everyone assumes they are the reality unless stated otherwise.

When individuals, communities, or organizations uncritically accept the existence of nonidentities, McRuer goes on to assert, they fuel a compulsion to achieve what Judith Butler calls a "phantasmatic idealization."[3] A phantasmatic idealization is an ideal—for our purposes, a bodily ideal—that most people cannot attain. Put another way, the ideal is simply a phantom. But in keeping with the allure of achieving normalcy, as we discussed in chapter 4, we attempt to maintain dominant or "normal" identities through constant and repetitive imitation of what we believe to be the ideal. Thus, compulsory able-bodiedness is the process whereby all of us—disabled or not—strive to attain the phantasmatic idealization of the nonidentity of the normal body.

Exploring a question that McRuer asks his readers to consider might help us better understand how some of the processes of compulsory ability work: "How many institutions in our culture are showcases for able-bodied performance?"[4] The arena of professional sport provides one example of a cultural institution showcasing able-bodied performance. In fact, in professional sports, hyperableism emerges as the standard as TV and radio commentators praise athletes for performances that go beyond reasonable physical limits while also critiquing performances that fail to achieve feats of extreme athleticism. Hyperableism in professional sports often intertwines with the maintenance of yet another nonidentity: hypermasculinity. The premium placed on competition emphasizes the codependency of power and performance and showcases the "ideal" male body as the normative player and performer.

Even in the arena of disability sports, which purports to celebrate the disabled body, athletes and commentators alike advertise their desire to mimic the hyperable, hypermasculine body that knows or shows no physical limitations. Extreme wheelchair or other disability sports are increasing in popularity. A quick Google search yields descriptions of programs and teams for wheelchair basketball, skiing with a disability, scuba diving lessons for people with disabilities, mountain biking for the blind, and more.

FIG. 2. One of the few photos of FDR with his wheelchair visible (Franklin D. Roosevelt Presidential Library)

Bloggers and trainers warn that you should not try these activities at home, and they declare that some of these activities are extremely dangerous. Proponents of extreme disability sports claim that the events ensure equal access and opportunity for people with disabilities to adventure, exercise, and participate in athletic competition, but they also inadvertently showcase compulsory able-bodiedness. A dogged pursuit of the "phantasmatic idealization" of compulsory ability fuels competitors' hunger to achieve hyperathleticism and hyperability—whether they are disabled or not.

In the United States, the political stage provides another vivid example of a cultural institution that showcases able-bodied performance. The age and health of political candidates are often topics of discussion as the public sorts through crowded fields of electable wannabes and pundits juxtapose the merits of youth and vigor with the perceived benefits of age and experience. The carefully choreographed public images and appearances of the United States' thirty-second president, Franklin Delano Roosevelt (FDR), provide one of the most glaring examples of how the political world asserts an able-bodied norm. FDR did not deny that he had a disability, but there is ample evidence that FDR and his cabinet skillfully avoided photographing the president and his wheelchair, thus removing the focus of the lens away from the president's disabled body. A caption for a photograph included in the photo spread in biographer and political scientist Jean Edward Smith's award-winning biography of FDR reads, "This photo, taken by Daisy Suckley, is one of only two images known to exist showing FDR in a wheelchair."[5] FDR ultimately completed four celebrated terms as president. One must ask, however, whether he would have been elected to his first or subsequent terms if FDR's wheelchair and disability had not been so skillfully obscured from public view.

Although seemingly disparate examples, professional sports and FDR's presidential career offer fertile ground for reflecting on how public institutions perpetuate, to borrow Butler's terminology, a phantasmatic able-bodied ideal, which demands constant and repetitive imitation to sustain itself. The examples of sports and FDR—one lionizing able bodies, the other shrouding disabled bodies in secrecy and denial—display remarkably similar patterns. Each in its distinct way publicly reproduces, asserts, and thereby showcases an able-bodied ideal, thus establishing able-bodiedness as the dominant nonidentity while simultaneously feeding a compulsion to mimic said nonidentity.

Another theoretical underpinning of crip tests comes from my friend and former colleague Glenn Bracey and his coauthored article with his colleague Wendy Moore, "'Race Tests': Racial Boundary Maintenance in White Evangelical Churches."[6] I first encountered the concept of "race tests" when Glenn joined the faculty at Hollins University, where I work. Glenn's office was next to mine in Pleasants Hall, so we enjoyed many impromptu hallway conversations about our respective research and writing. We quickly discovered shared research interests and passions. Glenn is a sociologist who focuses on the sociology of religion. I am a religious studies scholar who relies on sociological methods in my research. I was deep into my research on the experiences of people with disabilities in religious communities and organizations when I met Glenn, and Glenn's research at that time focused on racial boundary maintenance in white evangelical churches. Glenn and I found a lot to discuss!

I found Bracey and Moore's conception of race tests especially insightful, not only for making sense of how white evangelical organizations maintain whiteness as the dominant nonidentity, but also for understanding how many religious communities maintain able-bodiedness as the dominant nonidentity. In chapter 3, I noted the dangers of the logic of substitution, where one scholar substitutes their own analytical concept for a framework borrowed from another scholar. The danger is that when we separate a concept from its original context, we risk minimizing its original significance and impact. As I said in chapter 3, this is not my intent in using concepts from race to discuss disability. Bracey and Moore's writing makes important contributions and interventions in the sociology of religion as well as critical race theory, and I want you to look up their work and read it. The more Glenn and I talked, however, the more overlaps I noticed between Glenn's description of how race tests work and the experiences my disabled interviewees described.

Bracey and Moore define race tests as "performances by white individuals and groups, in the presence of incoming people of color; they are patterned racial microaggressions that deploy persistent racist stereotypes and/or histories of racial violence to preclude or precondition people of color's participation in predominantly white social spaces, such as evangelical churches."[7] Bracey and Moore identify two types of race tests: utility and exclusionary. Utility race tests test people of color's willingness to reinforce and serve the interests of white people, while exclusionary race tests are utilized to push people of color out of an organization if they are not willing to acquiesce to white people's interests. In other words, white people use utility race tests to determine whether people of color will conform to or disrupt the established racial hierarchy in social spaces, and if people of color do not conform but disrupt, those same white people use exclusionary race tests to force them out. Hence in using race tests, white people in evangelical churches maintain whiteness as the unquestioned dominant nonidentity, protect and preserve white emotional comfort, and ascertain which people of color are the "right" kind of people of color to allow into their fold.

Together, McRuer, Bracey, and Moore provide the scaffolding for my thinking on crip tests. My definition of crip tests grows out of McRuer's articulation of compulsory able-bodiedness, which establishes able bodies as the unquestioned nonidentity. Furthermore, in my experience, able-bodied folks in religious communities use crip tests in similar ways to how Bracey and Moore describe white people's use of race tests in evangelical churches. Thus, able-bodied people use crip tests to establish able bodies as the unquestioned nonidentity, to clarify that the emotional comfort of able bodies is the priority, and to communicate subtly yet powerfully how the "right" kind of disabled people look and behave. To put it another way, able-bodied people use crip tests to test if people with disabilities will maintain or challenge the able-bodied status quo and, if the latter, to keep them from fully integrating into the community.

Religious communities that are not comfortable with disability deploy crip tests through both practices and attitudes. Crip tests test whether disabled people submit to or confront ableist or exclusionary practices and attitudes. If people with disabilities submit to exclusionary and ableist practices and attitudes, the community welcomes them with enthusiasm. If, however, people with disabilities confront exclusionary and ableist practices and attitudes, the community withholds genuine welcome, making it clear that it prefers that people with disabilities remain silent or leave.

I know I keep repeating this, but once again, I want to acknowledge that most of the time members of religious communities do not intend to be exclusive or ableist. Nevertheless, this does not excuse exclusionary and ableist practices and attitudes. Let's delve into some examples of practices and attitudes that demonstrate how crip tests work.

We'll begin with a few practices. Ableist and exclusionary practices come in many forms, but one example is the extent to which buildings, bathrooms, or ritual and worship spaces are or are not accessible. Most of us assume that a community prioritizes access and inclusion when any combination of ramps, elevators, ASL interpreters, braille material, pew cutouts, or accessible bathrooms exists. Conversely, if there is no evidence of such accommodations, we assume the community is inhospitable and exclusive. Yet the mere presence or absence of literal physical alterations does not alone determine the extent to which a community prioritizes inclusion and access.

Religious communities may provide accommodations or "fixes," but sometimes these fixes are simply performative, intended to give the appearance of accessibility and inclusion without any serious commitment to actual disability justice. For example, a worship space may have pew cutouts for wheelchairs, suggesting a commitment to accessibility and inclusion. But a closer examination of the specific location of the pew cutouts may tell a different story. Are the pew cutouts at the front, in the middle, or in the back of the worship space? What message is communicated when pew cutouts are tucked away in the back corner of the room? How does the message change when they are in the middle or center of the space? What might a disabled newcomer surmise about a community's commitment to inclusion based solely on the placement of the pew cutouts?

The mere presence of accommodations does not guarantee access and inclusion, but the reverse is also true: The lack of physical alterations does not necessarily indicate exclusion. Remember Jonah's story of being carried up the synagogue stairs from earlier in the chapter. Even though the space was physically inaccessible, the community rallied to ensure that Jonah was fully included. In recounting this story, Jonah was adamant that the question was never *if* he would be included; rather, it was *how* he would be included. In contrast, the rabbinical school to which Jonah had been admitted was unable or unwilling to provide the necessary accommodations.

The synagogue and the rabbinical school each appear inaccessible, but because accessibility involves more than simply modifying physical spaces, Jonah and we can assume other people with disabilities feel included in some inaccessible spaces and excluded from others. Imagine now that you are a newcomer to Jonah's childhood synagogue, and one of the first things you witness is several members carrying a young boy in a wheelchair up the steps and into the building. What does this action indicate about inclusion and hospitality? What does this action indicate about a particular community's comfort with disabled people and disability? Does this example demonstrate a crip test?

New people would certainly notice the absence of a ramp, yet they also would notice a community ensuring that no one was left outside at the bottom of the stairs looking up at a sign proclaiming that "All Are Welcome." In this instance, new people would also notice that this is a community comfortable with disability and committed to access and inclusion. This is a community that does not appear to deploy crip tests.

The rabbinical school, in contrast to the synagogue, deployed a crip test. The school admitted Jonah and, in doing so, performed inclusion. Yet when Jonah showed real interest in attending, the school was unable—unwilling?—to provide the necessary accommodations. In this case, the crip test did not force Jonah out of the institution; it prevented him from going at all. The rabbinical school showed discomfort with disability by refusing to provide accommodations, even though Jonah was clearly qualified to attend. The crip test here tested whether Jonah was satisfied to be admitted without ultimately insisting on attending.

I don't know the end of Jonah's story with the rabbinical school. At the time of our conversation several years ago, Jonah appeared content to wait and see what happened. My sense was that Jonah did not harbor anger; he simply opted to channel his energy elsewhere. Another disabled person might have made a different choice and forced the issue with the rabbinical school, failing the crip test imposed by the institution.

To be clear, I am not suggesting that religious organizations (or any organization) ignore the importance of literal, physical access. A genuine commitment to disability justice requires spending the money and time to alter inaccessible buildings and provide the necessary accommodations to guarantee equal access whenever possible. There are nevertheless times when it is not feasible to alter physical spaces. Sometimes a community is open, in theory, to having people with disabilities in its midst, but not if it requires changing the status quo. The disabled person who wishes to pass the crip test and therefore gain access to the community must yield to the status quo. Alternatively, sometimes a religious community signals that it is willing to assume responsibility for cocreating an inclusive, hospitable, accessible, and welcoming environment by removing crip tests as a condition of participation, even if it might not be able to physically alter the space. Crip tests expose the ways a religious community regulates if, how, and to what extent a person with a disability is welcomed and included.

Like ableist and exclusionary practices, ableist and exclusionary attitudes also come in many forms. Exclusionary and ableist attitudes originate from long-held stereotypes about people with disabilities and histories of ableism. Crip tests based on exclusionary and ableist attitudes rely on histories of discrimination and oppression to ascertain if people with disabilities will quietly conform to ableist standards or boldly disrupt them.

As we noted with exclusionary and ableist practices, religious communities invoke crip tests, consciously or unconsciously, to ascertain and subsequently modulate to what extent people with disabilities will confront or conform to ableist and exclusionary attitudes. Likewise, religious communities already comfortable with disability either avoid or correct exclusionary and ableist attitudes when they pop up. Religious communities draw on ableist and exclusionary attitudes when they use crip tests to exert subtle yet persuasive control over which people with disabilities gain entrance into a community and, once they are in, if they can stay. I single out three exclusionary and ableist attitudes to explore that showed up most frequently as crip tests in my interviews: inspiration porn, the weaponization of prayer, and the disabled body as divine canvas.

Without exception, all of my interviewees talked about encountering some version of what the late journalist, comedian, and disability activist Stella Young called "inspiration porn."[8] In a blog post and TEDx Talk, Young described inspiration porn as "an image of a person with a disability, often a kid, doing something completely ordinary—like playing, or talking, or running, or drawing a picture, or hitting a tennis ball—carrying a caption like 'your excuse is invalid' or 'before you quit, try.'"[9] In her distinct Australian accent and with a dry humorous wit, Young quipped that the intent of inspiration porn is to give nondisabled people perspective on their own worries and lives. Inspiration porn enables nondisabled folks to tell themselves that things could always be worse. If that person with a disability can cheerfully live life and embrace challenging situations with a smile, the theory goes, so can I. Inspiration porn reduces people with disabilities to "exotic" others who provide stirring examples of how to live with difficulty, but they are not to be envied.

While Young explicitly defines inspiration porn as "images," the phenomenon manifests in a variety of ways. One of my favorite firsthand examples of being invoked as inspiration porn gives me the opportunity to toot my own horn! I am simultaneously a really good and obsessive knitter. In fact, I am one of the best knitters I know. I do, of course, make mistakes—every knitter does. I once showed my mom a sweater I had just finished, and she said, "Huh, I would not have thought to put those colors together." To which I retorted, "What two colors? This sweater is all one color!" Of course, my mom was right—there were two colors. When one ball of yarn ran out and I needed a new ball, I unknowingly picked up another ball that was the wrong color and knit an oddly placed L-shaped patch in the middle of the sweater! But this isn't the inspiration porn part—I had, in fact, made a mistake. Multiple color challenges aside, it's my ability to make beautiful garments with elaborate cables and patterns that tempts some people to highlight my accomplishments in ways that feel designed to highlight my difference.

I was working on one of these beautiful knitting projects while visiting my parents during a graduate school break. Several of my parents' friends joined us for dinner, and I knitted while we caught up over drinks before dinner. One of the friends noticed my knitting. I appreciate compliments on my knitting, but this man took complimenting to a whole new level. He banged on and on about how amazing it was that I could knit. "Oh, Darla, I just don't understand how you do that. You are incredible. I admire you so much. How you manage to knit without being able to see is beyond me." At this point in the book, you won't be surprised to learn that I have never been accused of being subtle. Having not yet encountered Young's fabulous talk, I did not have the language to articulate what I felt, but I recognized the unwelcome feeling of being othered. In my sweetest sarcastic tone, I quipped, "Well, I'm blind, not stupid." A brief pause followed, and then the whole room erupted into gales of laughter. Snippy retorts may not be the best response to being subjected to inspiration porn in most contexts, but in this case, my over-the-top admirer received the message with good humor.

Inspiration porn and controlling images often overlap in particular ways in religious communities. In communities of faith, inspiration-porn compliments take on a decidedly religious tone: "God has a special plan for you," or "You are a special angel," or "God sent you to teach the rest of us how to live with difficulty." Consider again reflections from Ella about saintly living, some of which I previously shared in chapter 3:

> I would sit around with these [disabled] friends of mine in high school, and we would talk about how annoyed we were that people think that we were all of a sudden these super-Christians because we go about living our lives right? . . . And we didn't have any language to talk about it. We didn't have a framework or context for it. It was just this sort of thing where it was, "Well, God bless you for living your life and for showing up to school and for keeping your faith during chapel or whatever." Looking back that sort of set off something for me. It's like I became really aware that Christians in particular look at me, and they, more often than not, assume that I'm some sort of saint, and not in the sort of generic definition of saint either. What does that look like when I walk into a new church or new worship community? I think a lot about how I'm perceived when I enter a new community. It gives me a lot of anxiety.

"Saint" is a common controlling image of people with disabilities, and this was also the most typical descriptor among my interviewees when discussing inspiration porn.

Although able-bodied folk who consciously or unconsciously invoke inspiration porn are almost always well intentioned, such statements come across to me as patronizing expressions of pity, ignorance, and fear. As Ella and Young point out, there is nothing especially amazing about doing ordinary things. Finding inspiration in someone with a disability managing basic life activities belies the attitude that disability equals inability. When able-bodied people add a layer of religious ideology and God talk to the mix, it cuts deep into the psyches and souls of people with disabilities.

The weaponization of prayer is another common crip test exhibiting ableist and exclusionary attitudes, particularly among more evangelical-leaning Christian denominations. Most of my

Christian interviewees did not generally object to intercessory prayer, which simply means the act of praying on someone else's behalf. They did, however, object to certain types of intercessory prayer. My interviewees rejected prayers that communicate negative attitudes about disability—for example, "Dear God, please remove this terrible affliction." They also did not appreciate it when well-meaning Christians forced specific prayers on them without their consent—for example, "Dear God, we pray for all people with disabilities that they may be healed." Finally, most of my interviewees did not welcome prayers focused on literal healing or cures: "Dear God, please restore Darla's full sight."

Melissa, a minister in the Presbyterian Church (USA) with mobility disabilities, labeled unsolicited prayer offered on her behalf as "bad theology":

> The only times that I run into problems are with some individuals who feel like they have to pray for me, "We'll pray for you to be healed." I tell people, I'm no longer praying for healing. I'm praying for patience; I'm praying for other things in the world. I'm praying to be able to do the job God's given me to do, but healing is not something that I'm praying for because I don't think it's in my cards. This is how I am. This is how I'm meant to be. And so don't pray for me to be healed, because I don't believe that's going to happen.

Lisa, a blind Methodist minister, shares Melissa's frustration with people who want to pray for her complete healing. She tells a humorous story that illustrates what happens when "bad theology" and the reality of disability collide: "I had one guy who was internationally known, more in the evangelical world, as a healer, and he anointed my eyes and prayed over me: 'Open your eyes. What can you see? Nothing? OK, well, let's pray again.' 'Open your eyes. What can you see? Nothing? OK, let's pray again.' He did it about four times, and finally it was like, 'OK, the Lord be with you.'" The stubborn persistence of Lisa's blindness befuddled the faith healer to such an extent that he tersely dismissed her, suggesting that if she would not be healed, he wanted her to go away.

Melissa's and Lisa's experiences demonstrate how prayer is weaponized in multiple ways to communicate a religious community's assumptions about disability and to regulate to what extent people with disabilities are (or are not) integrated into the life of the community. As Melissa's comments highlight, there are plenty of reasons to pray. If, however, the only petition offered on behalf of a person with a disability is for physical healing, the message is clear: Disability must be eliminated. If, however, the prayers request another form of "healing," such as patience, acceptance, or the knowledge to know how to practice genuine inclusion, a different story about disability can unfold.

Limiting prayer requests to physical healing in the face of disability not only reflects a lack of imagination and understanding about the expansiveness of the power of the divine but also denies people with disabilities the agency to celebrate the bodies in which they live, love, work, dance, play, pray, run, walk, stroll, roll, and so on. In other words, it denies people with disabilities the agency to celebrate living ordinary lives, doing ordinary things, in whatever body they inhabit. Moreover, limiting prayer requests to physical healing conveys a community's discomfort with disability and its desire to eradicate it.

Lisa's story may make us chuckle, but it unmasks a disturbing conundrum for the more traditionally faithful: How does one reconcile an absolute belief in the omnipotence of God as mediated through prayer with the stubborn persistence of disability? Lisa's so-called healer simply dismissed her without commentary or acknowledgment when it became clear that his prayers were not being answered. The response to unanswered prayer, however, is often more sinister than this. When intercessory prayer does not render healing, too often religious communities blame the person with a disability for lack of faith or for unforgivable sinful behavior. Rarely do they recognize that the problem is "bad theology." It is even less common for such religious communities to admit that the disabled person may not desire or need healing to enjoy a complete and fulfilling life.

Thus, when religious communities weaponize prayer, they are testing whether people with disabilities share the conviction that disability should be eliminated, agree to be prayed over, or assume the blame when, almost inevitably, healing does not occur. The extent to which people with disabilities comply with exclusionary and ableist attitudes of a religious community determines if, how, and to what degree they are "allowed" to participate.

The exclusionary and ableist attitude I refer to as "the disabled body as canvas" is the logical extension of the weaponization of prayer. The weaponization of prayer tests whether people with disabilities surrender to being objects of prayer, thereby assenting to the belief that disability should be eliminated. The disabled body as canvas tests whether people with disabilities exhibit the expected or "appropriate" (as defined by the community) response to the prayers. The canvas crip test, in other words, determines to what extent people with disabilities agree to serve as vehicles for the brilliant revelation of God's power if prayer results in literal physical healing. Or, if literal physical healing does not occur, the extent to which they interpret their ability to thrive regardless as evidence of God's power and goodness.

In chapter 3, I mentioned an article I cowrote with my friend Jennifer Koosed that focused on the story of the healing of the man born blind found in the Christian Gospel of John.[10] Jennifer and I presented an earlier version of this article at a session of the southeastern regional conference of the AAR when we were still graduate students. The session facilitator chose several papers for presentation and then invited a senior scholar to respond to the papers. I can't speak for Jennifer, but as a young budding scholar, the thought of a senior scholar commenting on our paper terrified me. The respondent was the late Dr. Hector Avalos, one of the early scholars in the field of disability and biblical studies.

I remember listening attentively to Dr. Avalos, but honestly, I don't remember many of the details. I think he commented on the basics of our argument and disagreed with a few of our minor points. Despite my fuzzy memory, one point Dr. Avalos made stuck with me over the years. He said, "What I find the most compelling and controversial about this paper is that Koosed and Schumm boldly question the linkage between the display of God's power and human suffering." Dr. Avalos then quoted our paper back at us: "In John 9, the implication is that God is using the man's blindness (which is characterized as an undesirable state that brings the man suffering) for God's own show of power. We question whether any link between God's will and human suffering is helpful, especially when God seems to be using the person for God's own (selfish?) purposes."[11] Dr. Avalos went on to ask the audience to consider not only the possibility but also the consequences of a selfish God who uses human suffering to display God's power. In that moment, I began to consider what it meant for my body to serve as a canvas for God's display of power.

When religious communities reduce disabled bodies to mere canvases to display God's power, they turn people with disabilities into passive vessels for divine play. Religious communities welcome people with disabilities into the fold because our bodies serve a purpose. Our bodies remind the able-bodied that, regardless of the outcome of intercessory prayer, the divine is in control.

Inspiration porn, the weaponization of prayer, and the disabled body as canvas function as crip tests that regulate if and how people with disabilities are welcomed and included in religious communities. Will people with disabilities acquiesce to serving as inspiration, objects of prayer, or canvases of revelation for their nondisabled counterparts? If people with disabilities quietly smile and carry on without confronting the patronizing attitudes expressed through inspiration porn, the weaponization of prayer, and the co-opting of disabled bodies as canvases, the community generally embraces them as "special" members who remind others to be grateful for what they have. If, however, people with disabilities adopt disability activist Eli Clare's mantra "Piss on pity"[12] or follow Stella Young's example and retort, "I do not want to be your inspiration porn,"[13] the loving embrace of the community may be withheld or withdrawn, and people with disabilities may feel unwelcome and excluded. When a religious community rejects and resists inspiration porn, the weaponization of prayer, and the reduction of disability to a canvas for showcasing God's power, we begin to discover a path for genuine access and inclusion.

When religious communities are not comfortable with disability, community members use crip tests to establish able-bodiedness as the unquestioned nonidentity, thereby casting people with disabilities as the "exotic other." Crip tests reinforce the idea of able bodies as the community norm, thus ensuring that rituals and practices—secular and sacred—are always organized around the presumption of able bodies. Moreover, through crip tests, religious communities ensure that the emotional comfort of the able-bodied is paramount. When religious communities are not comfortable with disability, they tolerate disabled people if and only if they serve an able-bodied agenda.

According to an article in *The Washington Post*, Batya Sperling-Milner read from the Torah as part of her bat mitzvah—the coming-of-age ritual for Jews—on a snowy Saturday morning in January 2019 at Ohev Shalom synagogue in Washington, DC.[14] There is nothing remarkable about a Jewish girl or boy reading from the Torah as part of a bat or bar mitzvah; it is the natural culmination of years of Hebrew study and preparation. A bar or bat mitzvah is the time when a Jew reaches the age of majority, or adulthood, halachically speaking (i.e., according to Jewish law).[15] Yet for Batya, who is blind, the act of reading from the Torah represented multiple triumphs. It not only signified the triumph of crossing the boundary from childhood to adulthood but, perhaps more importantly, also illuminated the dual triumphs of dismantling practical barriers to access and disrupting centuries of long-held rabbinical attitudes questioning whether blind Jews were fit to read the Torah for their communities during public services.

The first obstacle for Batya was the very practical question of how she would "read" the text. Reading the Torah includes identifying the "trope," the symbols included above or below the Hebrew letters that indicate how to read, sing, and chant the text. While preparing for her bat mitzvah, Batya discovered that there was no braille system for the trope. Further confounding the practical challenge of accessing the trope was the deeply held conviction, shared by Batya, her family, and their entire Modern Orthodox community, that making one mistake when reading even a single letter or singing a solitary note of the Torah violated Jewish law. Fortunately for Batya, the family had a friend living in Israel, a software engineer who was developing a system for inserting new braille characters for tropes into selected Torah passages. Simply print the respective passages with a braille printer and voilà!

The second obstacle demanded more fortitude and ingenuity. Batya and her family were confronted with the conundrum that some interpreters of Jewish law (but not all) assert that blind people "reading" the Torah by memorizing or using braille does not fulfill the obligation for public Torah reading for those in the audience. Batya was caught between her competing desires to celebrate her bat mitzvah—as instructed by Jewish law—and to abide by rabbinical teachings. In this case, Batya was fortunate to have a mother who is also a Jewish educator. Batya's mom wrote a forty-page paper arguing that blind people should be allowed to read from a braille copy of the Torah scroll during Jewish services and rituals, thus fulfilling the obligation of a public Torah reading. She further argued that the invention of braille Hebrew in the mid-twentieth century rendered the rulings of earlier rabbis obsolete. The letter continued a sacred Jewish tradition of interpreting and reinterpreting Jewish law, known as midrash.

On the day of her bat mitzvah, Batya's friends decorated her left hand with henna in the shape of the pointer that sighted people use when reading from the Torah scroll to avoid touching the sacred text. Commenting on Batya's revolutionary and revelatory Torah reading, the rabbi said, "Every single person in the synagogue showed up to hear her read, and we all felt we were in the presence of greatness."[16] As if to demonstrate that the divine has a wicked sense of humor, the Torah passage in the predetermined reading cycle for the day of Batya's bat mitzvah was about one of the plagues where God plunged the Egyptians into darkness so the Jews could flee. According to *The Washington Post*, Batya quipped, "It must be a sign from God!"[17]

A mother, a family friend, and an entire Modern Orthodox Jewish congregation rally to empower a blind thirteen-year-old girl to practice her faith and celebrate her bat mitzvah. Another Jewish community carries a young boy in a wheelchair up and down the stairs, enabling him to go in and out of the synagogue. What do these and undoubtedly other communities share in common? They all asked questions focused on *how*: How will we make our space more accessible? How will we include this person with a disability, even though our space may not be physically accessible? How can we transform as a community to reject exclusive and ableist practices and attitudes and to become inclusive, accessible, welcoming, and hospitable? How can we become more comfortable with the presence of disabled people in our midst?

These communities serve as models for bypassing crip tests. They did not allow physical or architectural barriers or discriminatory practices and attitudes to impede a commitment to fully welcoming and including all bodies in their midst. Most importantly, they collectively asked how. Instead of deploying crip tests, they demonstrated a commitment to dismantling ableism and practicing disability justice.

~ 6 ~

Slow Futures, Crip Time

"Do you think you will have twenty-twenty vision in heaven?" I've been asked versions of this question many times (versions because not all my friends believe in a Christian heaven). My answer: "I don't know, and I don't really care." While my flippant attitude usually cuts off further discussion, many of my interviewees also reported being asked this. It makes sense. Questions about the afterlife, or what happens after death, are a common theme across religious traditions.

The concept of a so-called afterlife mystifies me. In fact, I remember as a child singing a verse from the Christian hymn "Amazing Grace" that starts "When we've been there ten thousand years" and freaking out at the idea of being "there"—heaven—for ten thousand–plus years. I no longer believe in the literal Christian heaven of my Mennonite upbringing, but I do find some comfort in the idea of some form of existence after this life. What it is, I cannot say. I also don't spend much time fretting about it.

Ideas about the afterlife vary among religious traditions. The traditional Christian understanding of heaven includes streets paved in gold, with Jesus sitting at the right hand of God welcoming newcomers to their perfect eternal paradise, free from all suffering and sadness. Islam also describes the afterlife as a paradise, free of fear and sadness and full of spiritual and physical pleasures. Judaism presents a less cohesive concept of life after death. Some Jews believe in a paradise similar to the one in the Christian and Muslim traditions. Other Jews believe that "heaven" is a more perfect version of this world. And still other Jews do not believe in life after death at all.

Buddhists and Hindus believe in the concept of reincarnation, which is the cycle of birth, death, and rebirth into multiple lifetimes. Good or bad karma, which translates to action, propels humans from one lifetime to the next. Good karma in one lifetime ensures rebirth in an equal or better situation in the next life, while bad karma generally results in a lesser form of existence the next time around.

For Buddhism, the end of the reincarnation cycle is nirvana, or enlightenment. Buddhist enlightenment arrives when a practitioner fully understands the true nature of reality, resulting in freedom from all attachment and perfect knowledge and wisdom. Hindus similarly strive for release from the cycle of reincarnation. But in their case, the end of the cycle is called moksha, which means that one's essence reabsorbs into the whole of the universe. Thus, in both traditions, an individual human may be reborn into many, many lifetimes, with the ultimate goal of escaping the cycle of birth, death, and rebirth.

There are too many Native and Indigenous beliefs about the afterlife to do any of them full justice here. Some North American tribes believe that people go to a spirit world when they die, which usually is described as "perfect" and free from suffering. Other Native groups share something like the Buddhist and Hindu belief in reincarnation. Still others blend beliefs from Christianity to explain what happens when we die. These are just a few examples of how religious traditions explain the age-old question, What happens after death?

Even a cursory review of beliefs about the afterlife reveals a common theme: Life after this world will be perfect. Some religious traditions, especially Christianity and Islam, explicitly connect the theme of a perfect afterlife with the physical body. Both of these religions teach that the human body transforms after death and resurrects into a new form in the heavenly realm. While no religion claims to have the definitive skinny on exact details of the heavenly reality, Christians and Muslims assert with a fair amount of certitude that the physical and mental pain, suffering, and disability experienced in our earthly lifetime disappear in heaven.

With this background, it is understandable that many people in my predominantly Christian context ask me and other disabled people if we think we will be healed or cured in the next life. Most but not all of the people asking this question are able-bodied. This is an ableist question, and it always feels yucky. The question implies that the questioner believes that the answer is, or should be, yes. It makes me feel like there is something wrong with my current body and that any "perfect" world should not or does not include disability.

To be sure, not all people with disabilities share my feelings about a disability-free afterlife. Plenty of disabled people find great comfort in the promise of a body free from disability, especially those folks who live with constant or intermittent pain. Dorothy, one of my interviewees who described herself as a lifelong Christian and who lives with a variety of disabilities resulting from childhood polio, noted, "I look forward to heaven. I look forward to seeing what my new body will be like. I think I will probably not have to carry my crutch or my cane around or wear the brace." Likewise, when explaining his belief that the Qur'an teaches that disability is just a temporary test, Ibrahim (whom we met in chapter 3) enthusiastically asserted, "The other thing is that this test is temporary. It's going to end when you die and you go to the hereafter, where there is no sickness, in heaven. Disease doesn't exist."

I don't mean to disparage Dorothy's, Ibrahim's, or anyone's belief about the afterlife. I remember attending my Mennonite grandmother's funeral, where there was a lot of talk about her eternal heavenly home. Even though I don't believe in that type of heavenly home, I found comfort in the thought that some aspect of her spirit continued on and that she had not simply ceased to exist. Yet I find myself wondering why some religious traditions focus as much, if not more so, on the next form of existence as on this one and why they insist on perfect disability-free bodies in the next life. What's up with that?

Remember Norman from chapter 4? Norman's existence explains in part why able-bodied (and some disabled) people assume that there will be no disability in heaven. We already discussed how normalcy functions to determine proper ways of being in the world. The logical extension of a "normal" body in this world is a "perfect" body in the next world. We make every effort to achieve the norm and eliminate the abnormal in our current reality. Because this reality is flawed and imperfect, we don't even attempt to attain perfection. But the promise of paradise, of heaven, is perfection. Normal is no longer good enough. Normal is the best we can hope for right now, but perfect awaits us in a future existence.

It never really occurred to me to question the presumption of a disability-free future in heaven when I was growing up, but the idea of a Christian heaven, in general, always made me uncomfortable. Layers of "bad theology," coupled with unquestioned ableist assumptions, conditioned me to imagine a heavenly future wherein I was no longer blind. At the same time, it made no sense to me that any form of suffering in this existence would somehow pay off in the next world. But this is the message I took away from church, and even from some family and friends. Many of my interviewees also recounted stories where they were told that the reward for their suffering (read: disability) in the here and now would come in the form of a perfect, able body in heaven.

These messages, all of which promise perfect, whole, able bodies in heaven, contain multiple layers of ableism. For one thing, they communicate that disability is undesirable and that the "reward" for enduring the suffering of disability is a perfect, able heavenly body. I discussed earlier in the book why I find it problematic to equate suffering with disability. But what troubles me even more about the insistence that people with disabilities need only to bide their time until some future heavenly bliss is that it shifts the focus away from our current reality and toward some abstract future. Alison Kafer calls this type of focus the "forward-looking gaze."[1] The forward gaze promises a better future and is intended to help people—in our case, disabled people—wait out the bad stuff until the better stuff arrives.

Some concepts of heaven rely on a forward gaze. The logic goes something like this: Any form of suffering or discomfort can be endured in this life because a long-awaited future (heaven) will make all the suffering worthwhile. Your life might suck right now, but it will get better later, so you just need to wait out the crappy stuff. A continuous forward gaze holds people with disabilities captive to the allure of a better future.[2] The allure of a better future simultaneously reinforces the idea that my current disabled reality is inadequate and that there is little reason to try to make it better because "better" comes later. The implication that disability is the crappy stuff is problematic enough, but what I find even more distressing is what Kafer calls an "ethics of endless deferral."[3] Simply put, an ethics of endless deferral enables individuals and communities to justify inaction in the face of injustice because they believe that all ills—physical and social—will be rectified in a future time. Let me be clear about what I mean here by "injustice." I am not talking about the injustice of living with a disability. I am talking about the injustice of systemic oppression, discrimination, inaccessibility, exclusion, and so on. An ethics of endless deferral—a product of an unrelenting forward gaze characteristic of some conceptions of heaven—allows religious communities to rest comfortably in the knowledge that they do not need to expend energy addressing disability-related issues now because it will all get "fixed" in heaven.

Kafer's thinking on this issue gives me some language and concepts for articulating a critique of my childhood concept of heaven.

Constantly anticipating a better future and hence justifying inaction in the now rubs me the wrong way. But here's the thing: My critique of heaven does not acknowledge how complicated discussions of the nature of heaven can be, especially when they involve the belief systems of faithful practitioners. And if I am being really honest, my own thinking about the promise of a disability-free heaven is more complicated than my critique indicates.

Most people I know with disabilities are in fact held captive, at least a little, by the allure of a better (disability-free?) future. As I have said multiple times, I do not long for a cure. Yet I cannot deny that perfect vision holds great appeal. Hell, I would be happy with almost perfect vision! Does a heaven where I am no longer blind seem appealing? Of course. Am I counting on a disability-free heaven? Not at all. Does a heaven where I am still blind but where access and inclusion are the norm and discrimination and injustice do not exist also hold appeal? Absolutely. I am in equal parts not waiting for and not opposed to the possibility of a heavenly cure. This is yet another one of those paradoxes I cannot fully explain to my able-bodied friends.

The best language I have found to describe my thoughts and feelings about heaven or whatever awaits in the next realm comes from Kafer when she writes, "The value of a future that includes disabled people goes unrecognized, while the value of a disability-free future is seen as self-evident."[4] And there it is. The crux of my unease with most traditional descriptions of heaven is that the value of a world that includes disability goes unrecognized, while the value of a disability-free world is assumed to be self-evident. I don't feel the need to spend much time debating if disability exists in heaven or not. It's a futile exercise, impossible to predict. What I care about is the fact that most people assume that the most desirable, valuable, worthy future does not include disability. This is misguided thinking. More importantly, it is ableist.

It must be noted that religion is not the only culprit insisting on the ethics of endless deferral or a forward gaze. Technological and medical research also purportedly promises a better future. Reports of cures or medical advances, whether they loom someday soon or in the distant future, propel faith, not in an abstract divine being, but in the almighty contemporary god of science. The impulse is the same: This life, this body, is unsatisfactory, and some external entity will at some point in the future make it "better," "new," "whole," "perfect." From an ableist perspective, the allure of the forward gaze, whether rooted in religious or scientific faith, enables disabled people to endure their "suffering," armed with tenacious bravery and persistent hope for a better future.

So let me repeat: People with disabilities have value. Living with a disability affords a vantage point that brings value to any community. When I admit that there is some appeal in the idea of a disability-free future, this does not negate the fact that I believe that my disabled perspective brings value to a community. I wish that religious communities that believe in heaven would spend less time focusing on their forward gaze and more time focusing on access, inclusion, and justice in the present moment. But if a future heaven is an important part of your religious community's belief system, I hope you take a moment to consider alternatives to a heaven where all bodies are "perfect."

Nancy Eiesland was the first Christian theologian to place disabled experience at the center of theological reflection. Following in the traditions of feminist and Black liberation theologies, Eiesland constructed and wrote the first disability liberation theology: *The Disabled God: Toward a Liberatory Theology of Disability*.[5] I mentioned Eiesland in chapter 1 because it was the experience of reading her book that allowed me to imagine that disability could be more than my individual embodied experience. Eiesland showed me that disability was a category for theological and theoretical reflection. While my thinking about disability and disability theology diverged over the years from Eiesland's, I owe her a debt of gratitude for helping me think more expansively about disability and for introducing alternative forward-gazing images of heaven and God.

The title of Eiesland's book tells you everything you need to know to grasp the radical nature of her forward gaze: *The Disabled God*.

She dared to suggest that one could imagine a Christian God who not only did not reject disability but embodied it. Eiesland offered readers several pathways for imagining a disabled God and hence a heaven that included disability. Two images lingered for me—and by all accounts many other disability scholars—long after I finished Eiesland's book.

In a now iconic passage in her book, Eiesland describes an epiphany of arriving in heaven and finding God in a sip-and-puff wheelchair: "I saw God in a sip-puff wheelchair, that is, the chair used mostly by quadriplegics enabling them to maneuver by blowing and sucking on a straw-like device. Not an omnipotent, self-sufficient God, but neither a pitiable, suffering servant. In this moment, I beheld God as a survivor, unpitying and forthright. I recognized the incarnate Christ in the image of those judged 'not feasible,' 'unemployable,' with 'questionable quality of life.' Here was God for me."[6]

Eiesland also asks her readers to reconsider a more familiar image: the wounds that remained on the resurrected body of Jesus. The Christian story tells us that the Roman authorities tried and crucified Jesus next to other common criminals. The story goes on to report that three days after his crucifixion, Jesus rose from the dead and returned to his followers. Understandably, throughout history, Christians focused primarily on the miracle of Jesus's resurrected body. After all, this is the defining moment that sets Christianity apart from Judaism and Islam.

But it is precisely in the defining moment of the Christian story that Eiesland encourages us to pause and notice Jesus's literal, physical, postresurrection body. Eiesland shifts the readers' gaze away from the divine, whole, resurrected body and toward the human, wounded body of Jesus. Eiesland points us to the marks on Jesus's hands and feet left by the nails used to crucify him. She asks us to notice that this is an image of a body bearing the marks of pain and physical imperfection. It's a disabled body. And as the story goes, this appears to be the body Jesus inhabited when he ascended into heaven.

Together, the images of God rolling around in a sip-and-puff wheelchair and Jesus's wounded, resurrected body ascending into heaven disrupted my childhood idea of a heaven where disabled bodies magically transform into whole, perfect, able bodies. Eiesland's provocative images of a disabled God create space for a future that not only includes disabled people but recognizes their value. They call into question the self-evident nature of a disability-free future. A disabled God upends the traditional portrayals of heaven so familiar to me and most of my interviewees. These alternative heavenly possibilities invite people with disabilities into the community of believers who proclaim that they are created in the image of God. If I can imagine a disabled God, I am able to imagine that my disabled body is also created in the divine image.

As powerful as Eiesland's approach may be, I am not actually interested in insisting on a God with disabilities. If God exists, God transcends all embodied realities. The power of these images nonetheless lies in their insistence that there is a present and a future that not only includes but also celebrates disabled and able bodies. Eiesland's disabled God does not dictate a future with disabilities, but it creates room for a future that, paraphrasing Kafer, recognizes the value of a future that includes disability.

One of the unexpected joys of doing interviews for this book was making some new friends. In the early days of this project, I met Lauren Tuchman at a disability and theology conference. We had a brief conversation at the conference, after which I reached out to see if she was willing to be interviewed. She said yes! As with all the interviews I conducted for this book, Lauren and I spoke on the phone, and I used a smartphone application called TapeACall to record the interviews. We had a lively conversation that lasted over an hour and a half. I was so excited about our conversation—so I was devastated to discover that I had failed to hit the record button on the handy app. Nothing from the call was recorded. It took me almost a year to muster up the courage to contact Lauren again and ask if we could redo the interview. Again, she graciously said yes! Our second phone call was equally invigorating, and this time I was careful to hit the record button!

I depart from my practice of using pseudonyms for my interviewees in Lauren's case. Maintaining Lauren's anonymity is difficult because one of the remarkable details of Lauren's history is that she is the first ordained, blind female rabbi.

Lauren is blind due to retinopathy of prematurity. She has some light and movement perception in her left eye, but she describes herself as "functionally blind." Lauren was exposed to multiple religious traditions growing up because her mother's background was Roman Catholic and her father had Jewish roots. Lauren noted that neither parent practices their religious tradition in a significant way, but she described her mother as "very spiritual in her own ways." Lauren remembered learning about Judaism from her father as a child and noted that he instilled in her an understanding of the divine as "incorporeal, all-encompassing, and beyond us."

When Lauren and her brothers were young, their mother returned to the Catholic Church to give her children a sense of religious connection. As a child, Lauren participated in the Confraternity of Christian Doctrine, or what is commonly referred to as catechism, which provides religious education for children who attend secular or public schools. But Lauren told me that she never "meshed" with Christianity, even as a child. "And then I found that for a variety of reasons, Christianity just was not my path. And I was always interested in religion and spirituality and seeking," Lauren recalled. In her late teens, Lauren began seriously exploring Judaism as a spiritual home. Lauren deepened her involvement in and knowledge of Judaism throughout college, but she did not formally convert until she was pursuing a master's degree at the Jewish Theological Seminary. Lauren was ordained a rabbi in 2018.

Like Eiesland, Lauren also proclaims that people with disabilities are created in the image of God, but she arrives at her theological conclusion from a different starting point. Drawing from the Jewish tradition, Lauren asserts revolutionary claims about what it means to be created in the image of God. Anchored in the texts of the Torah, she begins at the beginning: Genesis 1:27: "So God created humankind in his [*sic*] image, in the image of God he [*sic*] created them; male and female he [*sic*] created them."[7] Lauren takes seriously the proclamation that God created all humankind—including disabled people—in God's own image. This is a radical theological statement wielding the power to dismantle inequitable, exclusive, and unjust systems and structures because it erases embodied hierarchy.

What does it mean for religious communities to begin with the premise that all humans are created in the image of God? What does it mean for religious communities to actively proclaim that no one replica of God's image is superior or inferior to another? The Genesis text does not include qualifiers stating that some bodies are created in the image of God, while other less desirable bodies are not. Yet as we have witnessed throughout this book, this is the resounding message that many people inhabiting nonnormative bodies receive from their religious leaders and communities.

Most if not all members of religious communities enthusiastically affirm that everyone is created in the image of the divine. At the same time, many of us casually assert values or beliefs without fully absorbing what actions are required if we truly mean what we say. As the old adage goes, actions speak louder than words. Too many of us with disabilities hear our religious communities say one thing but act in a different way. Loud words and proclamations feel empty when they are delivered off-handedly or without reflection about what they actually mean.

What would shift if religious organizations and communities genuinely and intentionally embraced the radical notion that every body is created in the image of God? Every body: the Black, brown, biracial, female, nonbinary, transgender, mentally ill, intellectually and developmentally disabled, fat, anxiety ridden, impoverished, working class, immigrant, non-English-speaking, blind, neurodivergent, wheelchair using, deaf, chronically ill, stinky, dirty, loud—all created in the divinely marvelous image of God. Perhaps if this were the starting point for religious communities, equity, inclusion, and accessibility would no longer be sidelined as the concerns of a few but instead be centered as the priorities of the whole. Perhaps each body would be celebrated for what it can do and not ignored because of what it cannot do. Perhaps the image of God would expand to include a wider variety of characteristics and attributes. When religious communities fully embrace the attitude that we are all created in the image of God and thus worthy, beautiful, complete, and valued, we can all begin to do the hard work of disrupting the fallacy of a divinely decreed embodied hierarchy.

The question of the nature of heaven and the afterlife is about a future time. As it turns out, I spend a lot of time considering the general concept of time. Time is one of those concepts that is both too abstract to comprehend and so concrete that people across cultures and historical periods generally agree on its meaning. For the most part, an hour equals sixty minutes in all languages and countries. When I tell a friend I will meet her in an hour, we share an understanding of what that means. Most of us take for granted the parameters of literal clock time. Time is time.

But for people with disabilities, time is more complicated than the sum of seconds and minutes on a clock or mobile phone. Time often becomes one of the most frustrating components of our day-to-day reality. It turns into another practical roadblock to access, inclusion, and equity.

A few years ago, I wrote an opinion piece about time for *Inside Higher Ed*—a daily online publication for college and university faculty, staff, and administrators.[8] The piece was called "It's Time for 'Crip Time,'" and in it, I critiqued the highly time-regulated hamster wheel that is the tenure-track pathway to promotion in higher education. I wrote about my struggle to achieve all the standard benchmarks on the prescribed timeline: six years for tenure and promotion from assistant to associate professor and another six years for promotion to professor. I confessed my frustration that no one understood how much harder this process was for me because of my disability. I acknowledged that I needed to prove to myself (and, yes, to everyone else) that I could hit the benchmarks despite my disability. I also admitted some trepidation about writing the piece because I did not want to come across as a whiner. After all, I talk and write a lot about how disability is not necessarily a negative experience, and I worried that readers would confuse honesty about my struggles with complaints about being disabled.

For the record, I did hit all the professorial promotion benchmarks in the standard time frame. But I did not write the article as an homage to my professional successes. Rather, I wrote the piece both to reassure other academics with disabilities that they are not alone and to offer some suggestions for how colleges and universities could approach the tenure and promotion process (and other policies and processes) differently.

I suggested that colleges and universities should consider adopting "crip time." The concept of crip time emerges out of disabled experience and acknowledges that people with disabilities often experience time and the demands of time differently from nondisabled persons. Crip time might mean needing to sleep longer or needing more breaks or naps during the day. Crip time might mean taking longer to cook or perform other daily domestic tasks, to get from point A to point B, or to reach professional benchmarks. Crip time means disappearing for days or months at a time because of health-related issues or canceling coffee dates at the last minute because we're having a health-related flare-up. Perhaps most relevant to my current reality, crip time might mean taking much longer to write a book.

Crip time centers on what my friend and disability activist, author, scholar, educator, and rabbi Julia Watts Belser calls "disability wisdom."[9] Disability wisdom is hard-won, embodied knowledge that simultaneously critiques ableist practices, systems, and structures and offers life-giving, inclusive, accessible, justice-oriented alternatives. Disability wisdom encompasses more than crip time, but crip time is a subset of disability wisdom.

Most of the disabled people I know, including myself, live in crip time. At the most basic level, this usually means that it takes us longer to complete daily tasks. I'm a good cook, and I love cooking, but I am a very slow cook. Do a thought experiment: How would cooking be different if you had to do it with your eyes closed? I can't quickly glance at a recipe to read the next step, so I often have to listen to the whole recipe every time I need to consult it. I label my spices with braille, which means that I have to feel many jars before I find the right one. I chop vegetables very slowly because I use my finger as a guide to measure where to chop, and, well, fingers plus sharp knives plus blindness often equals chopped fingers. More than once, I misjudged where a pan was on the stovetop or in the oven and accidentally touched a hot coil or rack, so I slowly and carefully felt my way around the oven. In short, a meal that takes a sighted person an hour to prepare takes me twice the time.

In addition to moving at a different speed than most able-bodied folks, those of us with disabilities also spend a lot of time and energy figuring out how to navigate a world set up for able bodies. Remember all my spice jars? Not only does it take me longer to find the right spice, but I also have to spend time figuring out how to cook in a world and a kitchen set up for people who can see. To the extent that it is possible, my kitchen is set up for a blind cook, but that, too, took literal and mental time to arrange. My point here is that crip time is multifaceted. It's not just about the time it takes to complete a task but also about how people with disabilities experience time and the emotional, mental, spiritual, and physical tolls it takes to try to keep up with the speed of able-bodied time.

I spent the first part of this chapter talking about conceptions of the afterlife, particularly how a forward gaze leads to an ethics of endless deferral. Consider how many of the words in the previous sentence pertain to time: "first," "forward," "endless," "deferral." Each of those words and the concepts or ideas to which they refer involve more abstract ideas about time. Religious communities that are committed to dismantling ableism must begin deconstructing abstract notions of time.

Part of this process involves proactively designing rituals, sacred or worship spaces, events, and social gatherings with crip time in mind. The keyword in the previous sentence is "proactively." Religious communities that are serious about dismantling ableism will not wait until a person with a disability requests accommodations or access. Instead, religious communities that are serious about access and inclusion will adopt crip time and other inclusive practices so that when disabled people show up, they immediately feel welcome.

Sometimes, adopting crip time means changing the literal pace of things, but it can also mean anticipating accommodation needs so that people with disabilities do not need to spend time and energy requesting them. Grace, a wheelchair user who I interviewed, described how she defined belonging and inclusion in a religious community, in part, based on the amount of time and energy she had to expend figuring out how to get back and forth to church.

During her first two years of college, Grace met her faith and spiritual needs by bouncing from one campus ministry service or event to the next. At the beginning of her junior year, a minister who she met through one of the campus ministry events reached out to her and asked how long it had been since she attended a Sunday service. Grace admitted that she could "count on one hand" the number of times she had attended a traditional church service since starting college. It was not that Grace did not want to attend regular Sunday services. Rather, as Grace explained to the minister, it was hard to figure out how to get from campus to a church, especially in the winter when ice and snow made it almost impossible to wheel around on sidewalks. It simply took Grace too much time and energy to get to a church. "Well," the minister said to Grace, "my family and I will pick you up if you want to go to church on Sunday. We'll pick you up and take you to church." "It was at that time," Grace reflected, "that I began to be meaningfully included in the life of a local church."

For several months, the minister and his wife took turns picking Grace up for church. Eventually, a few more people with disabilities heard about the church and started attending too. After six months of the pastor and his wife shuttling the small group of disabled folks back and forth to church, the congregation bought a small school bus equipped with a lift for wheelchairs: "They bought a small school bus, and they would go around and pick us all up and then drop us all off again. Fifteen or twenty people in the church got certified to drive the van. They all got their CDL [commercial driver's license]. It was really a beautiful thing."

Getting to church (or anywhere) without needing to ask for a ride may seem like a small thing to someone who can hop in a car and drive. But for those of us who must rely on the goodwill of others to get to and fro, the relief of not having to ask, of not having to think about it, of not feeling like a burden is hard to explain. As Grace said, "I felt like I literally didn't have to ask for anything. All I had to say was, 'Hey, this is going on, I want to go.' They would say, 'Great, when can we pick you up?' I didn't have to say, 'I really want to go to this, and here's what I need.' I just said, 'I really want to go to this.' And they said, 'OK, it's done. Let's go!'"

"It's done. Let's go." Those four simple words communicate a community's commitment to inclusion and crip time. They communicate that the entire community, not just disabled people, share responsibility for ensuring that all members are included. They relieve people with disabilities of the burden of time and energy that it takes us to figure out how we will participate in community rituals and events.

Grace's example focuses on the very practical question of transportation, but we could apply the philosophy behind those four simple words—"It's done. Let's go"—to any number of rituals or practices. Remember my Communion dilemma from chapter 4? What if I didn't need to figure out how to participate in that ritual? What if, when I entered a new religious space, someone came up to me and said, "Welcome. This is how we distribute Communion to people who have trouble accessing the Communion rail on their own. We invite you to participate in this way if you so choose." It's done. Let's go.

What if a religious community of any ilk invited someone with a speech impediment to read the sacred text during communal worship and, instead of treating it like a painfully slow and uncomfortable process, welcomed it as an opportunity to slow down and take time to carefully meditate and reflect on the words and their meanings? It's done. Let's go.

What if religious rituals built around sensory ability, such as the Hindu practice of darshan, where a practitioner must look into the eyes of the gods and goddesses to see and be seen by the divine, placed an equal emphasis on other sensory experiences so blind people could also feel fully included in the ritual? What if the smells of the incense, flowers, and food offerings to the deities or the sounds of the music accompanying the ritual were understood as equally valuable ways of connecting with the divine? It's done. Let's go.

I do not have an exhaustive or prescribed list for how religious communities might approach the practical work of "It's done. Let's go." Disability activist, artist, and writer Leah Lakshmi Piepzna-Samarasinha calls this work "care work" in her book by the same title.[10] Care work starts with the premise that we are interconnected and thus mutually responsible for caring for one another's needs. Care work grows out of the knowledge that some days I have the energy to care for you, while at other moments, I need you to care for me. Care work involves buying groceries for a friend who can't get out of bed; understanding when a friend cancels a coffee date; driving someone to church, work, or school; or walking at a slower pace so your disabled friend can also enjoy the hike.

No singular formula or specific type of care work is appropriate in every context. A formula does not necessarily make a community equitable, just, inclusive, or accessible. Care work means that each community must collectively find the best solutions for their specific context. In fact, I am less concerned about the specific solutions. My primary concern, rather, is that communities proactively commit to care work, to finding solutions. Just as important, communities must not wait until disabled or other marginalized people ask for solutions. Take the initiative to ask what we need. Do not wait for us to ask or do not assume our accommodation needs are met just because we have not asked. Better yet, if possible, have it done when we arrive so we can simply go.

Not long before the date of this writing, I was invited to speak at an Episcopal church for a mid-week series during Lent, the period of reflection that Christians observe in the forty days leading up to Easter. A group of about forty parishioners, mostly in their sixties and seventies, gathered in the fellowship hall to listen to me talk about religion, disability, access, and inclusion. It took several minutes for the facilitator to corral the group's focus away from the fabulous dark-purple-and-caramel velvet shoes with lavender-and-cream paisley laces I was wearing and back to the actual topic at hand. Eventually, they stopped swooning over my shoes and started listening to what I was saying!

I talked about many of the themes I write about in this book. Because it was a Christian church, I told them about my Communion dilemma. I asked them to consider what it felt like for a person who uses a wheelchair to roll into a worship space and find the only pew cutouts in a corner at the back of the church. As is often the case when I give talks like this, several people started talking at the same time as soon as I stopped speaking and invited questions. While they did have some questions—and not just about my shoes—most people had a story to tell about a time when they or someone they loved felt excluded or experienced a lack of access. Eventually, the facilitator dismissed us, and we went to another room to indulge in tasty treats and more conversation.

As I ate my brownie and drank lemonade, the group started discussing the inaccessibility of their sanctuary. Like many historic buildings, this church was designed for able bodies. The folks around our circle noted that some effort had been made to improve access over the years. At some point, an elevator had been retrofitted to address the fact that the only other way into the worship space involved climbing a long, steep flight of stone stairs. The sanctuary did include several rows of short pews that served as their version of cutouts, but not surprisingly, these were all located in the back.

I had to excuse myself from the conversation because Jonathan and I had a three-plus-hour drive home. But as I left the lively discussion, I heard the group plotting ways to improve access. One woman was pointing out that all the pews were movable, saying, "It really would not be hard to move the shorter pews to the middle or even front of the sanctuary." Another person noted that many parishioners were older and had trouble reading regular-size print. "It would be so simple," she mused, "to just print several large-print bulletins." They barely noticed me leaving because they were so engrossed in doing proactive care work. As I climbed into the car, I thought to myself, "It's done. Let's go."

Adopting crip time and committing to care work are critical to building just communities. But there is another deeper, less tangible ingredient to cocreating justice-oriented communities. It requires reorienting our entire way of conceiving time, speed, and the future. I find author, scholar, and educator Ellen Samuels's concept of slow futurity helpful for doing the heady work of reorienting and reconceiving our relationship to time.

In the article "Slow Time, Slow Futurity," Samuels connects the very ability to survive to slowness.[11] Samuels argues that slowness is neither a choice nor an imposition but a tactic. Samuels calls this tactic "slow futurity." Slow futurity is "grounded in the limitations and possibilities of bodyminds who cannot keep up with normative temporal structures. It provides a necessary framework to think about how we live and move and work in this ever-hastening world."[12]

Samuels goes on to argue that a necessary twin of slow futurity is "slow violence," a term Samuels borrows from Rob Nixon's book, *Slow Violence and the Environmentalism of the Poor*.[13] Slow violence is not limited to the dramatic forms of violence we typically associate with the word "violence." Slow violence happens out of public view, eroding one's mind, body, spirit, and soul slowly over time. The types of phenomena that constitute slow violence are often not defined as violence at all. Slow violence encompasses structures and systems that discriminate against, diminish, and destroy people, the natural environment, and other beings. It is a violence that manifests in poor health care, pollution, climate change and devastation, inadequate governmental policies and protections for the most at risk, and other similar structures that produce harm. As I sit in a beautiful library writing these words, my phone buzzes with a headline announcing that the Supreme Court just ruled on a case paving the way for South Carolina to uphold voting maps that disenfranchise Black voters: This ruling is an example of slow violence.

The messages my interviewees and I have received, internalized, absorbed, accepted, or rejected from our religious texts, leaders, communities, and theologies are forms of slow violence. Religious rituals and practices that we are told must be enacted in particular ways and on a strict schedule are forms of slow violence. A lack of public transportation that can take a wheelchair user who wants to attend church on a Sunday morning is a form of slow violence. The question "Do you think you will have twenty-twenty vision in heaven?" is a form of slow violence.

Slow futurity offers a response to slow violence. Samuels insists that slow futurity "is not, like crip time, an alternative mode of temporality."[14] Rather, slow futurity reorients our relationship to time and future. It allows us to count the pauses, the naps, the breaks, the "wasted" time as productive time, as necessary time, as valuable time, as not only life-giving but life-survival time.

Slow futurity is a heaven where God welcomes people at the pearly gates from a sip-and-puff wheelchair. It allows us to imagine a future that not only recognizes the value of disability but also does not seek to ignore or avoid the social, spiritual, structural, or individual injustices that accompany living with a disability. Slow futurity celebrates the value and struggles of living with a disability as forms of resistance, protest, and justice work.

I met Rebecca Spurrier, a liturgical theologian, over email. I can't remember exactly what prompted the email introduction or which of us initiated it, but the end result was that we arranged to have lunch the next time we were both at the AAR annual conference. During that lunch date, we discovered that we had more than just a shared interest in religion and disability. It turned out, for example, that we both have ties to Mennonite and Episcopal communities—a fairly unusual combination!

Several years after I met Rebecca, I picked up her book, *The Disabled Church: Human Difference and the Art of Communal Worship*.[15] The book chronicles Spurrier's ethnographic research, conducted largely through participant observation, at a church she refers to in the book as Sacred Family Episcopal Church in Atlanta, Georgia. It's a great book, and I highly recommend it! If you do pick it up, you'll soon discover that Sacred Family is not your typical church, especially not your typical staid, highly prescribed, must-stick-to-a-strict-sixty-minute-service Episcopal church. One of the characteristics that makes Sacred Family unique is that 50 percent or more of the attendees live with a mental illness diagnosis. Another unusual aspect of Sacred Family is that they place difference at the heart of who they are and of what and how they do things. Sacred Family does not try to conceal difference; rather, the church celebrates the different forms of human variation in all its messiness and beauty.

In the third chapter of the book, "Disrupting: Aesthetics of Time and Work," Spurrier observes that "there's a different sense of time in being here [Sacred Family]."[16] Disruption, Spurrier notes, is a primary feature of how events, services, and people move through time at Sacred Family. She describes how congregants pop in and out of services for a cigarette break or because they can't sit for long periods of time without feeling antsy. She notes how many conversations follow winding paths, veering from one seemingly unconnected topic to the next. Spurrier recounts one story where the man in charge of passing around the offering plate disappeared right before it was time to collect the offering and other people had to scramble to find him. She describes how congregants engage differently during a sermon: Some pay close attention, others fall asleep, still others wander around the sanctuary whispering to their friends as they walk past. These and many other stories describe a church community moving at a different speed of liturgical and community time.

Many of Spurrier's descriptions of Sacred Family capture the essence of crip time and slow futurity. This is a church where disruptions are not necessarily disruptive but rather expected and woven into the fabric of religious rituals and community. But Sacred Family is not a utopian community without conflict or uncomfortable moments. Sacred Family is a religious community where vulnerabilities are laid bare, where difference is not avoided, and where disruption often dictates the speed of worship and other communal gatherings. Sacred Family serves as one model of a religious community embracing crip time and slow futurity. It is not the only model, but it offers a starting point for religious and other communities to consider.

In embracing crip time and committing to care work, religious communities like Sacred Family begin building just communities. Delving deeper into the fabric of justice-oriented endeavors also allows us to embrace the radical notion of slow futurity. Slow futurity challenges us to reconfigure our relationship with time, speed, and the future, asserting that slowness is not merely a choice but an intentional reorientation to time. It encompasses the recognition that survival is intricately linked to slowness, offering a framework to navigate the relentless pace of our contemporary world.

Slow futurity presents a counterpoint to the violence of societal structures and systems that corrode individuals and communities over time, imagining a future where every moment, regardless of pace, holds significance and value. It is a future where the inherent worth of all individuals, disabled and able-bodied alike, is not only recognized but celebrated. Slow futurity invites us to imagine a world where resistance, protest, and justice intersect, where the rhythms of every life are honored, and where the journey toward equity, access, and inclusion is embraced.

Do I think I will have twenty-twenty vision in heaven? I don't know, and I don't really care. If heaven does exist, I imagine it operates on crip time. I imagine that heaven is a slow future where slowness is the standard pace of time. If my imagined heaven exists, my body will be perfect with or without twenty-twenty vision. But I do not want to spend my time waiting for that forward-gazing heaven. I do not want religious communities to spend their time spinning in an ethics of endless deferral waiting for that heaven. I want to spend our collective time creating that image of heaven in this moment, in this present, in this now.

~ 7 ~

Healing Ableism

In 1994 I moved to Nashville, Tennessee, to start a PhD program in religion, ethics, and society at Vanderbilt University. Unlike many of my PhD friends, I opted to complete a master's degree before applying to doctoral programs because I wanted to test the waters first. I needed to figure out if I had the personal and academic chops to pursue doctoral-level work. Turns out, I did! Truth be told, I was pretty confident I could handle it even before I matriculated into the master's program at the Pacific School of Religion in Berkeley, California, but I wondered what sorts of unique challenges would arise related to my blindness. During the master's program, I discovered not only that I had the chops to do graduate-level work but that I was more than capable of managing the blindness-related challenges, which ranged from keeping up with copious amounts of reading to finding alternative ways to take quizzes, tests, or exams.

So I moved to Nashville full of confidence and ready to tackle the PhD. Eight years later, I left with far less confidence, wondering if it had been worth the effort. I questioned if I had ever belonged there at all. What happened in those intervening years to squash my confidence and cause me to question my place in the academy?

The short answer is sexism and ableism. While there were other female students and we had a handful of women professors, women were still a significant minority in the academy when I matriculated into the PhD program in 1994. For example, I was one of only two women in a class of seven entering the religion, ethics, and society doctoral program that year. Having a cohort of nearly 30 percent women might not sound terrible, but at that time, all but one of the students already enrolled in the program were men, and the only two ethics professors were men. I immediately realized that finding a place in the academy as a woman was going to be an uphill battle. In the first five minutes of student orientation, I decided that Sally, the other woman in the program, and I needed to be friends, allies, and our own support group, whether or not we liked each other! Fortunately, we liked each other very much, and we remain close friends to this day.

As far as I could tell, I was also the only new student with a disability. Given current statistics about the number of people with disabilities, I feel sure, in retrospect, that I was not the only disabled doctoral student. Yet at the time, it certainly felt that way. My disability was particularly hard to hide, especially because I asked for volunteers—who got paid—to read to me in every class I took. I marvel now that I got through graduate school by relying on human readers to "read" the many philosophical and theological tomes my professors assigned. Today, a blind graduate student would rely on ebooks or audio versions, but these either did not exist or were much less available at the time. Instead of a screen reader, I had other students.

Word spread quickly among the other graduate students that there was a blind woman who needed readers. Reading for me was a great gig for other students because the university's disability services office paid them to read to me, which meant getting paid to do their homework, and many of my readers turned into lifelong friends. As a rule, my professors were supportive and accommodating as soon as I made my needs known. Nevertheless, I was deeply aware of my status as the only student with an apparent disability. Until my husband, Jonathan—who has a hearing disability—arrived on campus three years later, I knew no one else in the graduate school with a disability. At Vanderbilt, then, one of my first impressions was that no one else "looked" like me. I am not the first person to observe that it is hard to feel like you belong in a place or space where no one else's body looks like yours, be it in terms of race, gender, disability, or some other marker of minority identity.

Not long after I started at Vanderbilt, I had another experience that compounded my growing sense that maybe I did not belong in the academy. Within weeks of arriving in Nashville, I contacted the Tennessee Department of Vocational Rehabilitation (DVR). DVR is a government-run state agency in all fifty states, Puerto Rico, and the District of Columbia that assists people with disabilities in securing education and employment opportunities. My mom connected me with DVR when I was growing up in Indiana, and my experience there was generally positive. I attended some life-skill classes DVR offered when I was in middle school and high school, and the DVR agency assisted our family in identifying and purchasing visual aid equipment. I remember how excited I was when DVR staff delivered a closed-circuit TV (CCTV) to our house, which was a large magnifying unit complete with a TV screen monitor. I would slide a book or piece of paper under the magnifying glass, and the text would be projected in large print on the screen. This was, of course, when I could still read large print.

In Nashville, I contacted the Tennessee DVR because I was interested in purchasing some adaptive computer equipment and software for low-vision and blind people, and I wanted to learn more about some scholarship programs they offered. As is often the case with government services and agencies, the application process was tedious and involved. I was in my late twenties when I moved to Nashville, so I no longer had my mom around to do the grunt work connecting me to services. Several months after I submitted my application, I was relieved to learn that I had been assigned a case worker, and we set up a time for her to come to my apartment. I don't remember her name—let's just call her Mrs. Smith.

Mrs. Smith was a middle-aged woman, somewhere in her late fifties or early sixties. She struck me as someone worn down by a long career in social services. She wasn't exactly unfriendly, but neither was she warm and fuzzy. Mrs. Smith whipped out her clipboard, complete with the requisite paperwork, and started asking her questions: name, date of birth, address, and so on. It was all pretty standard stuff until she asked my highest education level. "I have a master's degree," I answered. At this point, Mrs. Smith stopped scribbling, looked up from her clipboard, and said, "You have a master's degree? I thought you were asking for assistance to get an associate's degree." I have no idea why she thought this, aside from the fact that many able-bodied people assume that people with disabilities do not, or cannot, earn postsecondary degrees. "No," I replied, "I am working on my PhD." "What?" Mrs. Smith said in an exasperated tone, "Why do you need a PhD? Someone in your situation should be satisfied with a master's degree; why on earth would you need a PhD?"

I initially had no response for Mrs. Smith. I was simply dumbfounded by her question. "Well," I stammered, "I plan to be a college professor, and I need a PhD to do that job." "Can't you just teach middle or high school?" Mrs. Smith persisted. By now, I was beginning to recover from my initial shock at Mrs. Smith's impertinence, and I snapped: "I don't want to be a middle or high school teacher, I want to be a college professor." I don't remember much about the meeting after that because I was so outraged by Mrs. Smith's attitude. She explicitly told me that I should be satisfied with the degrees I already had and implicitly suggested that I did not really belong in a doctoral program. For the record, I did receive some financial assistance from the Tennessee DVR, in spite of Mrs. Smith's attitude.

* * *

The words "belong" and "belonging" have become buzzwords at colleges and universities in the past few years. My own institution recently rebranded its student affairs division as Student Success, Well-Being, and Belonging (SSWBB) to convince prospective and current students that their well-being and sense of belonging are a top priority. Indeed, part of what crushed my spirit during my time at Vanderbilt was continually questioning if I belonged in that program or at that school. Many of my interviewees echoed similar sentiments, telling me that they felt they did not belong in the religious, educational, and other institutions with which they had been affiliated.

James, an African American Methodist minister who is visually impaired and experiences extreme light sensitivity because of a head injury from a car accident when he was a toddler, talked during our interview about how the intersections of racism, poverty, and ableism conspire to make disabled people of color feel as though they do not belong. James grew up in the 1970s and 1980s in what he described as a poor neighborhood in a large city in the Rust Belt. James recalled how doctors and educators predicted that he would never graduate from high school: "I can recall when I was starting school, because this is one of those benchmark moments for me, sitting outside my doctor's office. An educator from my school was there as well. I remember hearing—my parents didn't know that I heard this—but they told my parents at that time that 'you probably should not look forward to [James] graduating from high school with a diploma because people with his disability do not do well in integrated [meaning disabled and nondisabled children in the same classroom] school settings at all.'"

After much deliberating, James's parents decided to send him to the regular public school anyway, placing him in what is typically referred to as a "mainstream" classroom. James's parents advocated tirelessly for him, having to convince his teachers that he really did have a disability and that he needed accommodations. Despite his parents' efforts, James's teachers expressed frustration with what they perceived as their student's difficult behavior: "For about four years, I frustrated my teachers, but none like my fifth-grade teacher. I remember being in the fifth grade, and my teacher thought that I was lying. She would see me outside playing, not knowing how much it took for me to even be outside in the sunlight, but she would see me out there, and so she thought that I was just acting out in class because when it came time for me to read out loud, I would tell her I couldn't read it. She would get so irritated with me."

As the year went on and James continued to tell the teacher that he couldn't read from a book or the blackboard, the teacher's response became more aggressive. The teacher kept demanding that James read, and James kept insisting that he could not read: "She put me in the front row of the classroom. Then she said, 'OK, read it [the blackboard].' And I said, 'I still can't read it.' This woman picked me up in my chair, dragged me up to the front, put my chair next to her desk, and said, 'This is your seat for the rest of the year.' I did not know until years later that she put down in my record that I was acting out in class, that I was a behavioral problem. The next year they put me in behavior disabled classes."

Research demonstrates that Black and disabled children, especially boys, experience higher rates of in-school disciplinary action, suspension, expulsion, and referrals to law enforcement because of race- and disability-based implicit bias. Valerie Strauss, an education writer for *The Washington Post*, reported in a 2018 article that "students with disabilities and all boys also experienced disproportionate levels of discipline. But black students were particularly overrepresented: while they constituted 15.5 percent of public school students, they accounted for 39 percent of students suspended from school."[1] Strauss went on to note that two-thirds of students who have experienced all six common disciplinary actions (out-of-school suspensions, in-school suspensions, referrals to law enforcement, expulsions, corporal punishment, and school-related arrests) are boys, even though they represent just over half of all public school students. Furthermore, while only about one in eight public school students has a disability, one in four students referred to law enforcement, arrested for an in-school incident, or suspended from school is a student with a disability. Black students with disabilities and all boys with disabilities experienced a much higher percentage of these disciplinary actions.[2]

Strauss's article, which was based on data published in a report prepared by the U.S. Government Accountability Office (GAO),[3] exposed one of the most vexing social ills of our time: a racist, classist, ableist educational system that forms the scaffolding of what is sometimes called the school-to-prison pipeline, especially for Black boys and adolescents. James's story begins like the stories of so many Black disabled boys in America. After the fifth grade, James spent several years in the behavior disabled classes, where he only received remedial instruction. He spent most days in school playing cards with his classmates. But James's story did not end in that classroom or in prison. He told me, "I remember looking around one day, because one of my saving graces was that I was also in band and choir, so I was having conversations and hanging out with kids who were in college prep, accelerated, and genius classes. I remember thinking to myself, 'We think the same.' Then I remember sitting in the behavior disabled class one day, and I thought, 'I don't belong here.'"

James approached his principal and asked how to get out of the behavior disabled classes. The principal informed him that the only way to transfer into college prep courses was to test into them. James insisted on taking the tests, even though the principal discouraged him, expressing great skepticism about his ability to pass any of the tests. "I took the tests," James told me, "and when the results came back, I was college prep, except for math." From that point on, James enrolled in college prep classes, except for math. The system told James that he did not "belong" in college prep classes. James, in turn, showed the system that, in fact, college prep classes were exactly where he belonged. This would not be the last time that James was told that he did not belong in a community or space, but more about that later.

For now, let's return to a fact I briefly mentioned in the previous chapter about Rabbi Lauren Tuchman: Lauren is the first blind female rabbi in the United States. In my humble opinion, this should be an unremarkable statement because it should have happened many decades ago. But Lauren was ordained in 2018. Let me repeat: Lauren Tuchman, the first blind female rabbi, was ordained in 2018, just six years ago at the time I am writing this chapter. Defenders of the inclusiveness of Judaism may be quick to note that the first female rabbi was ordained in 1972, now over fifty years ago. Likewise, they might point out that Moses, one of the most revered biblical prophets whom God appointed the recipient and communicator of divine law, lived with a speech impediment (Exodus 4:10). Or they might observe that there have been blind male rabbis for so long that it is difficult to pinpoint an exact date for the ordination of the first male blind rabbi.[4] And both male and female rabbis with a variety of other disabilities have been ordained for many years. When contextualized alongside these other facts, one could conceivably argue that it is neither remarkable nor indicative of underlying discrimination that the first female blind rabbi was ordained only six years ago.

Yet I contend that the fact that there were no blind female rabbis before 2018 communicates to people with disabilities that they do not fully belong in some religious communities, even if they can boast some examples of disabled leaders. Lauren's initial attempt to apply to seminary, for example, was met with ableist attitudes and discrimination. The first seminary she hoped to attend disinvited her from applying after her initial campus visit. In the email disinviting her application, the institution asked, "How are you going to be able to read?" The question referred to the large amount of course reading expected of graduate students. Lauren was a college graduate with a master's degree; she had already successfully negotiated the challenges of blindness and reading in academic settings.

The ableism in the seminary's question not only brought into bold relief the discriminatory attitudes embedded in the institution but also communicated that Lauren did not belong there. For Lauren, it was a painful reminder of the emotional and spiritual injury religious institutions sometimes inflict. "It was a real rupture because they [the seminary] claim to be so progressive," Lauren recalled. Lauren's comments succinctly capture how experiences of blatant exclusion and discrimination in religious organizations leave lasting emotional and spiritual scars for people with disabilities. "So when I got that email and they said, 'How are you going to be able to read?' I was like, this game is over. I was already so traumatized by this completely unjust and ignorant experience."

The language of trauma may seem extreme when used to refer to being rejected from a graduate program. After all, many people are rejected from colleges and graduate programs. But when that rejection is based on overt discrimination against an aspect of one's immutable identity and when the rejection denies entry into a program where one hopes to gain the necessary training to live out one's vocational calling, the language of trauma is apt. In a study of the psychological effects of discrimination on people with disabilities, psychologists Brian Watermeyer and Leslie Swartz note that this form of "social trauma" is often internalized, adding another complicated layer to living with disability: "It is necessary to understand how the disabled minority is used as a container for the unwanted, projected feelings of the dominant, as well as drawn into unconscious complicity with marginalization. . . . Trauma is visited on the lives of many disabled people in ways which are both acute and chronic, overt and subtle."[5]

Lauren went on to reflect on how the lingering scars from her traumatic experience with the first seminary haunted her presence at the seminary that did, without question, accept her into its program. Lauren's insightful description captures well what many of my other interviewees also described when talking about the cascading consequences of social trauma resulting from ableist institutional attitudes and practices:

And because I had entered rabbinical school frankly quite traumatized from the [first seminary] experience, everything felt very conditional. So I got to JTS [Jewish Theological Seminary], and my brain was telling me, "Just make sure you get through the next five years and just do whatever you can to get through." I do not believe that is how the institution saw me at all. I actually think that the institution would have been very willing to help me out in any way I needed, but I also was coming in with a fear of, "If I ask too much . . . ," and "too much" is a relative term, then I'm going to be asked to leave, which never ever ever came up. But it was just what my really traumatized brain was telling me. That's one of the things I really had to sit with since I graduated. What are the ways in which that really hampered me? You do the best you can with what you have at the time, but that doesn't mean that you don't wish you had the resources to do things differently.

Lauren's reflections underscore how social trauma often functions in the lives of people with disabilities. We are socially and culturally conditioned to believe that we must be grateful for whatever scraps we are offered. James's experiences, too, show why disabled people have reason to believe that if we ask for or expect "too much," we will be further marginalized and dismissed as demanding, unreasonable, difficult, problematic, whiny, ungrateful, a troublemaker, and so on. Social trauma from one experience informs subsequent experiences. When one institution discriminates against an individual or a group of individuals on the basis of their identity, those discriminated against carry those experiences and feelings of fear, inadequacy, and marginalization with them to the next institution. As Watermeyer and Swartz note, "Surviving in a world which continually questions one's belonging, leaves little personal resources for debunking oppressive social phenomena."[6] Even if another institution does not enact the same ableist attitudes, practices, and policies, the underlying anxiety that results from lingering social trauma is often incapacitating, affecting people's ability to advocate for their needs.

Lauren graduated from seminary and became a rabbi. James transferred to college prep classes, graduated from high school, and went on to college and graduate school. I persevered in the doctoral program and earned my PhD. Many people with disabilities also meet their personal and professional goals. But we must ask, Do institutions (whether religious or otherwise) actively anticipate and provide support for people with disabilities in ways that fully include them in the life of the community and allow them to achieve their goals? Do institutions make erroneous assumptions about what people with disabilities can and cannot do or do and do not need? Do institutions passively wait for people with disabilities to self-advocate for their access needs, or do they preemptively implement systems, practices, policies, and structures ensuring belonging and full inclusion? What are some strategies that religious institutions and organizations can employ to guarantee disability justice, inclusion, access, and belonging?

In chapter 1, I invited readers to join me in raging against ableism. I hope by this point you understand why I find ableism enraging and why I aspire to cultivate a community of people who join me in raging against it. Perhaps by now you feel some of this rage too. But rage alone only gets us so far. And while I believe that rage is a necessary and reasonable response to injustice, it is not the only necessary component for developing strategies for guaranteeing disability justice, access, inclusion, and belonging. Our raging must be accompanied by an equally strong desire for healing.

When I say "healing," I do not mean healing in the sense that most of us conceive of it. I am not talking about healing the disabled body or any body. Rather, I am talking about healing ableism. I am reminded of a line from writer Johanna Hedva's essay, "Sick Woman Theory," where Hedva turns the concept of "fixing" upside down: "You don't need to be fixed, my queens—it's the world that needs the fixing."[7] Paraphrasing Hedva, I say to all people with disabilities, You don't need to be healed, my friends—it's ableism that needs the healing. So I want to reissue my original invitation and invite you—disabled and able-bodied alike—to join me in the love work of raging against ableism and to also join me in healing ableism. But what does our raging and healing love work entail? How might religious communities, in particular, approach the work of raging against and healing ableism?

I believe that one simple phrase captures the spirit of this work: accessible love. But here it gets a little complicated. The phrase itself might be simple, but the concept is a little elusive. In some ways, the easiest way for me to tell you what accessible love means is by explaining how hard it is to define! Accessible love cannot be boiled down to a few concrete terms; accessible love is not a stable or stagnant concept or set of practices; accessible love shifts and changes depending on the situation, community, or individual needs and realities.

In this way, the trouble with defining accessible love mirrors the trouble with defining disability: It is difficult to capture the full scope of disability experience because it is so varied and diverse. Likewise, we cannot definitively say that accessible love means X or Y, but we can cultivate attitudes and practices that guide the work of implementing accessible love in specific contexts. Accessible love emerges as a fluid and flexible response to exclusionary and oppressive attitudes and practices directed toward nonnormative bodies. The power of accessible love is that it is action in motion; accessible love demands constant attentiveness to the access, inclusion, and belonging needs of all bodies in any given community. Accessible love is an orientation toward justice; it orients our hearts, attitudes, and practices toward inclusion, access, and belonging.

The kind of "love" I have in mind is not the romantic kind but the kind that disability performance artist, activist, and writer Leah Lakshmi Piepzna-Samarasinha has described as a "radical form of solidarity, called love."[8] For Piepzna-Samarasinha, solidarity, access, and love intertwine in ways that make it impossible to talk or think about one without the other. Likewise, the Reverend Dr. Martin Luther King Jr. and author, activist, and professor bell hooks situated their theoretical and practical justice work in revolutionary notions of love, particularly the idea of a beloved community. King's idea of beloved community insisted that we advocate for public policies rooted in compassion and caring and focused on driving out hunger, poverty, bigotry, and all forms of violence. hooks elaborated on what would be necessary to realize the dream of beloved community: "Beloved community is formed not by the eradication of difference but by its affirmation, by each of us claiming the identities and cultural legacies that shape who we are and how we live in the world."[9]

Theologian Kerry Day also defends love as a critical component of justice work and boldly asserts that "love is a concrete revolutionary practice."[10] Day argues that "love grounds an affective politics, which is a cultural politics of emotions that seeks to align the emotions of political subjects with certain political causes and commitments."[11] Building on hooks, Day contends that love involves both concrete actions toward others, such as affection, care, compassion, and mutuality, and the ways that "we fashion political communities and implement policy programs."[12] Day calls the type of love described by hooks (and others)—the kind where love moves from love for the self outward to others—"neighbor love." This kind of love can ignite a call to justice for all.

Neighbor love insists on a practice of love that embraces genuine compassion and empathy for the other and simultaneously demands that we extend this compassion and empathy to the other who is most different, foreign, or alien to us. For many of us, our initial response to the neighbor who is most different from us is what Day calls "projective disgust."[13] Day defines projective disgust as "a disgust for a group of other humans who are segmented from the dominant and classified as lower because of being (allegedly) more animal."[14] The power of projective disgust is that it is used as a "key tool of subordination and oppression."[15] All too often, people with and without disabilities regard disabled bodies as "more animal," repulsive, disgusting, or monstrous.

Day argues that genuine neighbor love repels projective disgust by mobilizing responses on both personal and political levels. Neighbor love, Day insists, is more than a cozy feeling toward the familiar. Neighbor love confronts feelings of disgust and simultaneously propels individuals and groups to confront the oppression of the most marginalized—the monstrous, repulsive, disgusting other. For religious communities and organizations, neighbor love is also rooted in an impulse to connect with the divine. Neighbor love is grounded in understandings and experiences of divine love and a deep desire to be present to God and the world at the same time.

I follow in the wake of Piepzna-Samarasinha, Dr. King, hooks, Day, and others who center love as the cornerstone of justice work. The scaffolding of accessible love comes from practicing genuine neighbor love, celebrating each person's distinctiveness, relying on compassion and care as guiding principles for developing political and public policies, and commingling solidarity, access, and love. As a praxis for subverting ableism, accessible love is firmly rooted in the messy spaces of embodied realities where bodies encounter one another: the material and built environment, unjust structures and systems, and discriminatory attitudes. Accessible love combines radical beliefs and practices. Accessible love is the radical belief that all bodies are worthy and deserve to be valued and included. Accessible love is a set of radical practices that ensure that all bodies enjoy full inclusion, accessibility, justice, and belonging.

Let's return to some examples of how the work of accessible love might unfold. Lauren's and James's stories highlight some of the ways ableism persists in religious and other communities and organizations, but their stories also suggest how religious and other communities might approach the hard work of accessible love.

As a rabbi, Lauren devotes much of her time and energy to community organizing and disability education and justice. She writes, lectures, leads workshops and discussions, and grants interviews for Jewish communities striving to transform into more just, equitable, inclusive, and accessible spaces. In an ELI Talk (the Jewish version of a TED Talk), Lauren draws from a moment in the Torah that centers on justice and inclusion. In the talk, titled "We Were All at Sinai: The Transformative Power of Inclusive Torah," Lauren observes that all of the Israelites were included at Sinai when Moses received the divine law (Ten Commandments) from God (Exodus 19–24).[16] All the Israelites received the divine law from Moses; all the Israelites entered the covenant with God. No Israelite was left out. God did not single out a privileged few who were expected to receive and follow the commandments. God did not exclude any body from the expectations or protections of the covenantal relationship. The covenant moment at Sinai established the standards of radical inclusion and participation in the life of the community. If, as Judaism and other theistic religions maintain, humans should imitate God in all things, then it is incumbent on religious communities to mimic the divine posture of radical inclusion as established at Sinai.

Earlier in this chapter, I wrote about the social and spiritual trauma that results when people feel they do not belong. People with disabilities can only feel they belong to a community if and when they are truly included or when the respective community practices radical inclusion. Too often, a community assumes that the work of radical inclusion is done once the physical spaces have been modified. But people with disabilities probe beneath the polished surfaces and uncover the communal attitudes that do or do not buttress a commitment to equity, inclusion, belonging, and accessibility. A religious community's deeper dedication to radical inclusion is quickly apparent, regardless of the condition of the building. The reverse is also true: A beautiful, accessible building cannot mask a community's lackluster approach to radical inclusion or disability justice.

Throughout this project, I spoke with disabled people who told me about their experiences in religious communities that gave lip service to inclusion and perhaps even adjusted their buildings and spaces but failed to reorient their attitudes toward radical inclusion. Ella articulated what many of my interviewees experienced when she said, "The spaces where I have felt the most welcome are the spaces where people have reached out and they have said, independent of me beating my head against a wall, 'We really want you here.' 'I really want you to participate in X. How do we make that happen?'" When Ella spoke about the community that said to her, "We will find a way to include you even though the space is not particularly accessible," her community exhibited accessible love by imitating the divine posture of radical inclusion as established at Sinai.

Religious communities that are serious about accessible love do not settle for surface-level inclusion. Religious communities that are serious about accessible love insist on radical inclusion, which means that the full participation of every member is an unquestioned value and guaranteed.

Like Lauren, James also blends his work as a religious leader with disability activism and advocacy. The story that I am about to recount is yet another one about ableism and discrimination, but its power lies in James's response, which also gives us another example of how to practice accessible love. After he graduated with a master of divinity degree (MDiv—the degree needed to be ordained in most Protestant Christian denominations), James declared that he wanted to be a pastor. Each religious tradition or Christian denomination has its own distinct processes for vetting, training, and accepting candidates for the ministry or religious leadership. The process in the United Methodist Church (UMC, James's denomination) involves multiple steps, including interviews with clergy, bishops, and ordaining boards as well as a field placement in a church.

The process did not flow smoothly for James: "During the probationary period—well, even before I got to that point, after graduating from seminary and declaring that I wanted to get certified as a pastor—I would make it until one point before being considered for going on to commissioning. I kept getting sent back to my local district, to the board of ordained ministry." James did not initially understand why he kept getting stalled in the process. Eventually, another clergyperson discovered what was happening and reported back to James: "I found out later that there was one pastor who kept blocking me because he did not see how I could serve effectively as a pastor as someone who is blind."

Faced with blatant ableism and being told yet again that he did not belong, James got creative. "When I realized who the pastor who kept blocking me was, I made it my business to get into his life," James told me with no malice. As a candidate for ordination, James needed another pastor to serve as his mentor. James knew that his adversary's wife was also a pastor. With a hint of a smile in his voice, James said, "I asked if this pastor's wife would be my mentor, which meant that he [the adversary] was at every event that I ever did because I would invite my mentor, and she brought her husband!"

James went on to tell me about one of the events that his mentor and husband attended. James organized and led a disability awareness forum for a local church called Beyond Accessibility. After the event, James's skeptic approached him with tears in his eyes and said, "I am so sorry. I did not know." "If you didn't know the background," James mused, "you would think that he was saying that he didn't know all of the things about the difficulty that people with disabilities go through in the ordination process or the way they are treated in churches, like always being on the periphery. He probably didn't know about any of that. But he was also saying that he did not know that I could do an activity like that. From that moment on, he has become my greatest advocate." In a much quieter tone, James reflected, "So it's changing hearts, changing minds."

Accessible love involves "changing hearts, changing minds" about people with disabilities. James changed the heart and mind of his adversary by exposing him to and educating him about disabled people's experiences of exclusion and discrimination. Let me hasten to add that just as it is not the responsibility of people of color to educate white people about racism, neither is it the responsibility of disabled people to educate their able-bodied counterparts about ableism. James embraces disability activism, advocacy, and education as part of his vocational calling; hence, this is part of how James practices accessible love. But not all people with disabilities want to be in the role of educator, nor should they be expected to be.

Observing James in action was perhaps even more effective for changing his skeptic's heart and mind about people with disabilities. Truly learning to know someone with a disability or who is different from us in any way is often the most powerful antidote to -isms and -phobias like ableism, racism, transphobia, homophobia, and so on. When you are different from me and we become friends, my heart and mind change; this is accessible love. We must all be open to having our hearts and minds changed about the people we deem different from us.

Once James was finally certified as a pastor, he incorporated principles of accessible love into his work as a minister. I asked James, as I asked all the clergy I interviewed, how he preached about sacred texts that portrayed disability in a negative or problematic way. In James's particular case, I asked him, "How do you preach about the healing narratives of Jesus?" At first, James just laughed. But then his tone turned serious. "To some extent," James admitted, "I run to them. My understanding of what the healing really was about is not that it was about healing the specific person in the story. These stories are not about showing that this person needed to be healed because they were lacking or cursed. The stories are there to show the community that it was missing out if it excluded the person with a disability." "What does your congregation think about your interpretation?" I asked James. "Well," he chuckled, "they already know that I'm not going to give the same reading that they're accustomed to. They know that I'm going to challenge those old theological groundings and make them more contextual."

Accessible love challenges "old" ideas, attitudes, mindsets, theologies, practices, and rituals—the list could go on. Accessible love means that we are not afraid to name an injustice, inequity, or form of discrimination, even if we find it in our sacred texts. Accessible love confronts oppressive structures, systems, and institutions. Accessible love is unsatisfied with ableist actions and attitudes. Accessible love rejects ableism. In these ways, accessible love changes and challenges individual hearts and minds, but it also changes and challenges oppressive and discriminatory systems, structures, institutions, theologies, rituals, and sacred texts.

* * *

Throughout this book, I have sprinkled suggestions for how those of us in religious communities can practice accessible love. These suggestions can apply to other types of communities and organizations as well. For example, I discussed how important it is to find inclusive alternatives to ableist language and metaphors. I recommended replacing damaging and negative controlling images such as the sinner, saint, or supercrip with the more capacious and positive image of the misfit. I gave some practical tips for designing more accessible and inclusive spaces and rituals, including making room in the center or front of the worship space for wheelchair users and serving Christian Communion to people who cannot get to the altar rail first. I asked religious communities to become aware of the crip tests they employ and to commit to finding ways to avoid or bypass them. I suggested adopting crip time as a strategy for moving at a slower pace and for realizing slow futures.

All these examples provide a snapshot of how accessible love drives our collective work of raging against and healing ableism. I have offered other examples throughout the book. But I have no desire to provide an exhaustive list or to prescribe a specific formula for practicing accessible love. The good and bad news is that there are no quick and easy formulas to solve the problem of ableism; there are no exhaustive lists for raging against and healing ableism. The lack of concrete guidelines may feel frustrating, but the freedom of not being tied to a specific formula means that each community can collectively discover, dream, and create its own formula for raging against and healing ableism—for practicing accessible love.

I have one last request for communities that are ready to take up the mantle of accessible love. Please ground this work in what has become a common motto within the disability rights movement and activist communities: "Nothing about us without us."[17] "Nothing about us without us" provides a succinct leadership blueprint for religious communities practicing accessible love. Almost every conversation I have ever had with disabled friends, colleagues, and interviewees eventually turns to a discussion about how well-intentioned able-bodied folks earnestly but often misguidedly problem-solve accessibility and inclusion issues without consulting disabled people. I am confounded by the regularity with which this happens across institutions, individuals, groups, and even families. More often than not, able-bodied people miss the accessibility mark because they attempt to solve the wrong "problem" or they propose a solution that does not in fact address the issue. Those of us with disabilities are the experts on our accessibility needs; solutions will be most effective if those most impacted participate in or lead the problem-solving charge.

You may not be shocked to read that along with one last request, I need to name one final paradox or tension. Earlier in the book, I said that religious communities should "proactively" strategize and implement accessibility solutions. In fact, I insisted that religious communities should do this work so that people with disabilities felt welcome and included as soon as we arrived. And now I am contradicting myself by requesting the opposite: Nothing about us without us!

But another earlier point applies here: Two things can be true at the same time. The first true thing is that I cannot overstate the relief that those of us with disabilities feel when we arrive to a space or community where access and inclusion already exist, where we immediately belong. The second true thing is that we need to be included in access and inclusion work; we do not want to be sidelined or ignored. If a community prioritizes disability accessibility, inclusion, and belonging work to the point that it is engaging in it even before disabled people are part of the community, that community must find ways to include disabled people in that work. Find people with disabilities to partner with. If the work is about disability access, inclusion, or belonging and we're already there, don't do it without us.

I must confess that sometimes I feel a little fatigued by the overuse of the words "belong" and "belonging." I might even say I find them sort of irritating. A psychoanalyst might reasonably speculate that my irritation with these words indicates a deeper concern or feeling about what it means to belong. Do I find these words annoying because they have morphed into empty buzzwords, tossed about without much thought or intent? Yes. Am I fatigued by the words "belong" and "belonging" because I often feel like I don't belong? If I am honest, the answer is also probably yes, especially when it's asked about educational, professional, and religious spaces and communities. In most cases, I can attribute those feelings of not belonging to ableism.

I have not let my sense of not belonging stop me from barging into these spaces and communities. I am fortunate in this sense because I am stubborn, goal oriented, strong willed, and most importantly, surrounded by an amazing and supportive network of friends, family, and colleagues. I do not let people like Mrs. Smith get in my way or keep me from pursuing my dreams. I listen to the Dr. Falls in my life, the people who tell me that I can do anything I want to do, except maybe drive a car.

And yet I live with a bone-deep fatigue from feelings of not belonging, of living with the constant feeling that I must prove that I belong. Over and over again, my interviewees told me that they, too, shared my feelings and fatigue.

It took me a long time to figure out that the source of my fatigue and feelings of not belonging arose not from my imperfect, abnormal, different, monstrous, and disabled body but from ableism. It took me a long time to believe that I do not need to be healed. Eventually, I figured out that my disabled body is normal, powerful, and beautiful. I know, without a doubt, that it's not me or any body with a disability who needs to be healed. It's ableism that needs the healing. If we practice accessible love together, we will successfully rage against and heal ableism. Please join me in the raging and healing work of accessible love.

Acknowledgments

Every author knows that they will accidentally leave someone out of the acknowledgments. Typically, they apologize for this at the end of the acknowledgments, but I want to start with that apology. I have been working on this project for close to a decade, and so many people have contributed to the book in big and small ways. I know I cannot possibly list all of you in a few short pages. Hence if your name does not appear in the next several paragraphs but you supported me along the way as I worked on this book, please know of my deep and abiding gratitude for your support, love, and friendship.

In my mind, there are two women without whom I truly could not have finished this book: Anne Amienne and Audra Wolfe. I first connected with Anne Amienne, the founder and director of Scholars and Writers, in 2018. For the first several years, I worked one-on-one with Anne, reestablishing a regular writing routine, setting goals, and banishing the negative writing speak in my head. As I have said more than once to Anne, when I met her, the thought of writing made me feel nauseous. After working with Anne for six years, the thought of not writing every day makes me feel nauseous. Anne quite literally helped me turn my dread of writing into a love of writing. Grateful barely scratches the surface when it comes to how I feel about Anne and her coaching support.

Another gift Anne gave me was introducing me to Audra Wolfe, an editorial and publishing consultant and founder of the Outside Reader. When I decided to take my project in a new direction, Anne suggested that I might find it useful to work with a developmental editor. To be honest, I was not entirely sure what a developmental editor offered, but I decided to give it a go. My first exposure to Audra was in a writing workshop. I liked her approach, but she intimidated me a little bit. I had heard that she was direct, tough, and gut-wrenchingly honest. Audra is all of those things, and she was exactly what I needed to take my messy and unorganized draft to the next level. Audra's advice and editing suggestions proved invaluable as I wrote my book proposal, chose a publisher, revised my messy draft, and wrote the final chapters of the book. I quickly got over being intimidated by Audra, and I eagerly anticipated her witty and direct feedback on my chapter drafts. Because Audra is tough and direct, I knew I could trust that when she told me my writing was good, she meant it. Thank you, Audra, for cheering me on and helping me find the confidence to finish a book. Thanks also to Julia Skinner, who also works with Scholars and Writers, for doing the "polishing" work on the manuscript, especially formatting and checking the citations.

After working with Anne for a few years, she recommended that I transition from one-on-one coaching to group coaching. I have participated in three iterations of Scholars and Writers coaching groups. We meet weekly over Zoom, and despite my intense dislike of Zoom, with each iteration of these writing groups, I experienced a profound sense of community. I cannot thank these women enough for their encouragement, virtual hugs, suggestions, and vulnerability as we struggled together to figure out how to write books while balancing the demands of teaching, administrating, parenting, partnering, and just trying to live and survive. Thank you especially to my current group, Jeanette, Jill, Joy, Vanessa, and Ximena. You all accompanied me across the book-writing finish line, and I will be forever grateful.

Thank you to Cindy Bohland, Giuliana Chapman, Kim Halsey, and Amy Hatheway, my "book" group (we have not read a book together in over five years), for making me laugh, solving problems I did not know I had, and being constant sources of love and support. Thank you to my dear friend Bethany Murphy, who is always up for an adventure and who helped me brainstorm the title for this book on one of those adventures.

My heartfelt thanks to LeeRay Costa, Lori Joseph, and Julie Pfeiffer, who have been part of my Hollins University "posse" for over twenty years. Julie and I have written, presented, and traveled together. I am indebted to Julie for teaching me how to be a better writer and for being an amazing thought partner, sounding board, and friend for all things writing related as well as for life in general. LeeRay and I started working at Hollins on exactly the same day, and I do not exaggerate when I say that I would not have survived these past twenty years without her. Lori ranks among my most faithful and loyal friends, and more than almost anyone, she has cheered me on and believed in me. My thanks to Laurie McLary, who only recently arrived at Hollins but quickly became a beloved friend and colleague. Laurie helped me find a few extra weeks during two summers, enabling me to devote uninterrupted time to finishing the manuscript.

In many ways, the seeds for this book were planted when I was in graduate school at Vanderbilt University. The friends I made at Vanderbilt witnessed the many ups and downs of my intellectual journey, and they buoyed me at every point along the way. My thanks to Anthea Butler, Rebecca Greene, Michael Stoltzfus, and Minette Watkins for helping preserve my sanity as I navigated coursework, comprehensive exams, and a dissertation. A very special thanks to Sally Holt, Jennifer Koosed, and Melissa Stewart, who have patiently listened to me ruminate about writing (and many other issues) for decades. I am not sure I would have ever published anything without the encouragement and support of Jennifer, who is my first and most frequent coauthor.

Although it is a cliché, there really is nothing like old friends. Thank you from the bottom of my heart to the triumvirate who have known me longer than most people in my life: Tina Birky, Nancy Chupp, and Deb Smucker. We have been friends since the ninth grade, and we still make it a priority to get together regularly. The three of you know all my flaws and secrets, and you still love me. I appreciate that for years, you asked about the progress of the book and immediately dropped the subject when I said it was too stressful to discuss. I also appreciate how enthusiastically you all cheered when I finally said, "Please ask about the book. I am ready to talk about it." The older I get, the more I value the gift of these lifelong friendships.

Thank you to the editorial, production, and marketing teams at Rutgers University Press. I am especially grateful to my editor, Carah Naseem. I appreciated Carah's energy and insight from the first time we spoke, and it has been a true joy to work with her. Thank you, Carah, for finding exactly the right balance between giving me the freedom to write the book I wanted to write and providing excellent feedback and editorial advice. Thank you to my production editor, Vincent Nordhaus, and the entire production team. Thanks also to Hannah McGinnis, the associate editor and project manager at Scribe Inc., for helpful copyedits.

This book would not exist without the generosity of time and insights of my interviewees. While I cannot name them individually because I promised anonymity, they all graciously gave me at least an hour of their time, and in many cases more than an hour. A simple thank-you does not seem adequate for your willingness to talk with a stranger about deeply personal experiences and feelings. It is my hope that our combined stories help heal ableism in religious and other communities. Thank you all for allowing me to include your story as part of this work.

I received two grants that enabled me to focus on research and writing during my sabbatical. Thank you to Hollins University and the AAR, respectively, for awarding me the Cabell sabbatical and AAR research grants.

Thank you, thank you to my parents, Clare and Katie Ann Schumm, and my brother, Ryan, for always believing in me. To understand how amazing my family is, you will need to read the book. Finally, no words express the depth of my love and gratitude for the two leading men in my life: my husband, Jonathan Harris, and our son, Henry Schumm. Jonathan and Henry keep me humble, make me laugh, and bring love, fun, joy, and excitement to every day. I love you both more than you know.

Notes

1. Introduction

1. Gail Pheterson, "Alliances Between Women: Overcoming Internalized Oppression and Internalized Domination," *Signs: Journal of Women in Culture and Society* 12, no. 1 (1986): 148, https://doi-org.hollins.idm.oclc .org/10.1086/494302.
2. Beverly Wildung Harrison and Carol S. Robb, *Making the Connections: Essays in Feminist Social Ethics* (Boston: Beacon Press, 1986).
3. Lama Rod Owens, *Love and Rage: The Path of Liberation Through Anger* (Berkeley: North Atlantic Books, 2020).
4. "The 2020 Census of American Religion," Public Religion Research Institute, last modified July 8, 2021, https://www.prri.org/research/2020 -census-of-american-religion/.
5. Judith Heumann and John Wodatch, "We're 20 Percent of America, and We're Still Invisible," *New York Times*, July 26, 2020, https://www .nytimes.com/2020/07/26/opinion/Americans-with-disabilities-act.html.

2. Let's Talk About Disability

1. "Disability Impacts All of Us Infographic," Centers for Disease Control and Prevention, last modified May 15, 2023, https://www.cdc.gov/ disability-and-health/articles-documents/disability-impacts-all-of-us -infographic.html?CDC_AAref_Val=https://www.cdc.gov/ncbddd/ disabilityandhealth/infographic-disability-impacts-all.html.
2. Centers for Disease Control and Prevention, "Disability Impacts All of Us Infographic."

3. "Guide to Disability Rights Laws," U.S. Department of Justice, Civil Rights Division, last modified February 28, 2020, https://www.ada.gov/resources/disability-rights-guide/.

4. U.S. Department of Justice, "Guide to Disability Rights Laws."

5. For one of the earliest articulations of the distinction between the medical and social models of disability, see Michael Oliver, *The Politics of Disablement: A Sociological Approach* (New York: St. Martin's Press, 1990). Tom Shakespeare addresses many of the debates within the field of disability studies in his book *Disability Rights and Wrongs Revisited*, 2nd ed. (New York: Routledge, 2014). Lennard J. Davis's edited collection, *The Disability Studies Reader*, 5th ed. (New York: Routledge, 2017), is one of the best and most comprehensive texts for use in college classrooms, but it is also an excellent introduction for any reader to the salient histories, themes, and controversies in disability studies.

6. Alexa Schriempf, "(Re)fusing the Amputated Body: An Interactionist Bridge for Feminism and Disability," *Hypatia* 16, no. 4 (2001): 60, JSTOR, https://www.jstor.org/stable/3810783.

7. Alison Kafer, *Feminist, Queer, Crip* (Bloomington: Indiana University Press, 2013).

8. Rosemarie Garland-Thomson, "Feminist Disability Studies," *Signs: Journal of Women in Culture and Society* 30, no. 2 (2005): 1557, https://doi.org/10.1086/423352.

9. Rosemarie Garland-Thomson, "Misfits: A Feminist Materialist Disability Concept," *Hypatia* 26, no. 3 (2011): 592, JSTOR, https://www.jstor.org/stable/23016570.

10. Michel Foucault, "The Subject and Power," *Critical Inquiry* 8, no. 4 (1982), accessed July 5, 2024, https://www.journals.uchicago.edu/doi/abs/10.1086/448181.

3. Sinners, Saints, Supercrips, and Misfits

1. Martin Luther, "Let Your Sins Be Strong: A Letter from Luther to Melanchthon," Project Wittenberg, accessed July 23, 2024, https://www.projectwittenberg.org/pub/resources/text/wittenberg/luther/letsinsbe.txt.

2. Patricia Hill Collins, *Black Feminist Thought: Knowledge, Consciousness, and the Politics of Empowerment*, 10th ed. (New York: Routledge, 2000).

3. Alison Kafer, "Compulsory Bodies: Reflections on Heterosexuality and Able-Bodiedness," *Journal of Women's History* 15, no. 3 (2003): 81.

4. "Adults with Disabilities: Ethnicity and Race Infographic," Centers for Disease Control and Prevention, September 16, 2020, https://www.cdc .gov/disability-and-health/articles-documents/infographic-adults-with -disabilities-ethnicity-and-race.html?CDC_AAref_Val=https://www .cdc.gov/ncbddd/disabilityandhealth/materials/infographic-disabilities -ethnicity-race.html.

5. "Kimberlé Crenshaw on Intersectionality, More Than Two Decades Later," Columbia Law School, last modified June 8, 2017, https://www .law.columbia.edu/news/archive/kimberle-crenshaw-intersectionality -more-two-decades-later.

6. All biblical quotes are taken from the New Revised Standard Version of the Bible (NRSV).

7. Jennifer Koosed and Darla Schumm, "Out of the Darkness: Examining the Rhetoric of Blindness in the Gospel of John," *Disability Studies Quarterly* 25, no. 1 (2005), https://doi.org/10.18061/dsq.v25i1.528.

8. Andy Calder, "'God Has Chosen This for You'—'Really?' A Pastoral and Theological Appraisal of This and Some Other Well-Known Clichés Used in Australia to Support People with Disabilities," *Journal for Religion, Health and Disability* 8, no. 1/2 (2004): 12.

9. Centers for Disease Control and Prevention, "Adults with Disabilities."

10. Christine James, "Catholicism and Disability: Sacred and Profane," in *Judaism, Christianity, and Islam: Sacred Texts, Historical Traditions, and Social Analysis*, ed. Darla Schumm and Michael Stoltzfus (New York: Palgrave Macmillan, 2011), 167–185. James borrows the phrase "moral ecology" from American legal scholar, political philosopher, and public intellectual Robert George.

11. James, "Catholicism and Disability," 167.

12. James, "Catholicism and Disability," 177.

13. James, "Catholicism and Disability," 179.

14. Gerard Goggin and Christopher Newell, "Fame and Disability: Christopher Reeve, Super Crips, and Infamous Celebrity," *M/C Journal* 7, no. 5 (2004), https://doi.org/10.5204/mcj.2404.

15. Eli Clare, *Exile and Pride: Disability, Queerness, and Liberation* (Durham, N.C.: Duke University Press, 2015), 2–3.

16. Edward Said, *Orientalism* (New York: Penguin Random House, 1979).
17. John 19:17–18.
18. Garland-Thomson, "Misfits," 591–609.
19. Garland-Thomson, "Misfits," 592.

4. Challenging Normalcy

1. Rosemarie Garland-Thomson, "Staring at the Other," *Disability Studies Quarterly* 25, no. 4 (2005), https://doi.org/10.18061/dsq.v25i4.
2. Garland-Thomson, "Staring at the Other."
3. Lennard J. Davis, "Introduction: Disability, Normalcy, and Power," in *The Disability Studies Reader*, 5th ed., ed. Lennard J. Davis (New York: Routledge, 2017), 10.
4. Tobin Siebers, *Disability Aesthetics* (Ann Arbor: University of Michigan Press, 2010).
5. Ann Millett-Gallant and Elizabeth Howie, "Disability and Art History Introduction," in *Disability and Art History*, 1st ed., ed. Ann Millett-Gallant and Elizabeth Howie (London: Routledge, 2016), 3.
6. Erwin Pokorny, "Bosch's Cripples and Drawings by His Imitators," *Master Drawings* 41, no. 3 (Autumn 2003): 293–304.
7. Heather Vacek, *Madness: American Protestant Responses to Mental Illness* (Waco, Tex.: Baylor University Press, 2015).
8. Cotton Mather, as quoted in Vacek, *Madness*, 18.
9. Cotton Mather, as quoted in Vacek, *Madness*, 18.
10. Vacek, *Madness*, 18.
11. One might reasonably ask if this man considered legal intervention based on discrimination under the ADA (Americans with Disabilities Act). It is important to note that while general employees of religious entities enjoy the protection of the ADA under Title I, the law provides a "ministerial exception." The ministerial exception applies only to people who conduct religious activities such as overseeing rituals, religious education, or worship. Thus, consistent with the First Amendment to the Constitution, which limits government intervention in religious organizations, ministers do not enjoy the protection of Title I of the ADA. For more information, please explore "Religious Entities Under the

Americans with Disabilities Act," ADA National Network, last modified 2018, https://adata.org/factsheet/religious-entities-under-americans -disabilities-act.

12. Carrie Sandahl, "Queering the Crip or Cripping the Queer? Intersections of Queer and Crip Identities in Solo Autobiographical Performance," *GLQ* 9, nos. 1–2 (April 2003): 25, https://doi.org/10.1215/ 10642684-9-1-2-25.

13. Shayda Kafai, "Crafting Disabled Sexuality: The Visual Language of Nomy Lamm's 'Wall of Fire,'" in *Bodies in Commotion: Disability & Performance*, ed. Carrie Sandahl and Philip Auslander (Ann Arbor: University of Michigan Press, 2005), 179.

5. Crip Tests

1. "What Is Universal Design?," UD Project, accessed June 6, 2024, https:// universaldesign.org/definition.

2. Robert McRuer, *Crip Theory: Cultural Signs of Queerness and Disability* (New York: New York University Press, 2006).

3. McRuer, *Crip Theory*, 9.

4. McRuer, *Crip Theory*, 9.

5. Jean Edward Smith, *FDR* (New York: Random House, 2008).

6. Glenn Bracey and Wendy Moore, "'Race Tests': Racial Boundary Maintenance in White Evangelical Churches," *Sociological Inquiry* 87, no. 2 (May 2017): 282–302.

7. Bracey and Moore, "Race Tests," 282.

8. Young first introduced the phrase "inspiration porn" in a July 2012 Australian Broadcasting Corporation (ABC) Ramp Up blog, and the concept gained even more exposure in her 2014 TedX Sydney Talk. Stella Young, "We're Not Here for Your Inspiration," Ramp Up, last modified July 2, 2012, https://www.abc.net.au/rampup/articles/2012/07/02/3537035 .htm; Stella Young, "Inspiration Porn and the Objectification of Disability: Stella Young," TedXSydney, https://youtu.be/SxrS7-I_sMQ?si= _3uaPgS2KuwC2_-4.

9. Young, "Inspiration Porn and the Objectification of Disability."

10. Koosed and Schumm, "Out of the Darkness."

11. Koosed and Schumm, "Out of the Darkness."
12. "Supercrip and the Politics of Pity," Serendip Studio, last modified September 8, 2014, https://serendipstudio.org/oneworld/identity-matters -being-belonging-becoming/supercrip-and-politics-pity.
13. Young, "Inspiration Porn and the Objectification of Disability."
14. Michelle Boornstein, "A Bat Mitzvah Girl Debuts a New Way for Blind Jews to Participate in an Ancient Tradition," *Washington Post*, January 14, 2019, https://www.washingtonpost.com/religion/2019/01/14/bat-mitzvah -girl-debuts-new-way-blind-jews-participate-an-ancient-tradition/.
15. Bar/bat mitzvah marks adulthood for Jews who both do and do not find halakhah binding. For example, Orthodox Jews find halakhah binding, while Reform Jews generally do not.
16. Rabbi Shmuel Herzfeld, as quoted in Boornstein, "Bat Mitzvah Girl Debuts a New Way."
17. Boornstein, "Bat Mitzvah Girl Debuts a New Way."

6. Slow Futures, Crip Time

1. Kafer, *Feminist, Queer, Crip*, 29.
2. Kafer, *Feminist, Queer, Crip*, 2.
3. Kafer, *Feminist, Queer, Crip*, 29.
4. Kafer, *Feminist, Queer, Crip*, 2.
5. Nancy Eiesland, *The Disabled God: Toward a Liberatory Theology of Disability* (Nashville, Tenn.: Abingdon Press, 1994).
6. Eiesland, *Disabled God*, 89.
7. Gender and queer studies scholars challenge the notion that there are only two genders and propose a more expansive approach to understanding gender construction.
8. Darla Schumm, "It's Time for 'Crip Time,'" *Inside Higher Ed*, June 26, 2022, https://www.insidehighered.com/views/2022/06/27/adopt-crip -time-make-higher-ed-more-inclusive-opinion.
9. Julia Watts Belser, *Loving Our Own Bones: Disability Wisdom and the Spiritual Subversiveness of Knowing Ourselves Whole* (Boston: Beacon Press, 2023).
10. Leah Lakshmi Piepzna-Samarasinha, *Care Work: Dreaming Disability Justice* (Vancouver: Arsenal Pulp Press, 2018). The concept of care work

grew out of early feminist writing and theorizing that proposed an "ethics of care" as one counterpoint to the production-focused system of capitalism. Early feminists such as Carol Gilligan, Joan Tronto, Nel Noddings, and Fiona Robinson argued that care labor was critical to a capitalist economy and thus should be valued and monetarily recognized. Care labor, or care work, as it is often called, emerged as a critical framework for feminist philosophers, economists, and theorists. Hence Piepzna-Samarasinha did not invent the phrase but borrowed it from feminists and other thinkers concerned with justice and equity.

11. Ellen Samuels, "Slow Time, Slow Futurity," *Panorama: Journal of the Association of Historians of American Art* 8, no. 1 (Spring 2022), https://doi .org/10.24926/24716839.13275.

12. Samuels, "Slow Time, Slow Futurity."

13. Rob Nixon, *Slow Violence and the Environmentalism of the Poor* (Cambridge, Mass.: Harvard University Press, 2011).

14. Samuels, "Slow Time, Slow Futurity."

15. Rebecca F. Spurrier, *The Disabled Church: Human Difference and the Art of Communal Worship* (New York: Fordham University Press, 2019).

16. Spurrier, *Disabled Church*, 100.

7. Healing Ableism

1. Valerie Strauss, "Implicit Racial Bias Causes Black Boys to Be Disciplined at School More Than Whites, Federal Report Finds," *Washington Post*, April 5, 2018, https://www.washingtonpost.com/news/answer -sheet/wp/2018/04/05/implicit-racial-bias-causes-black-boys-to-be -disciplined-at-school-more-than-whites-federal-report-finds/.

2. Strauss, "Implicit Racial Bias."

3. "K-12 Education: Discipline Disparities for Black Students, Boys, and Students with Disabilities," Government Accountability Office, last modified March 22, 2018, https://www.gao.gov/products/gao-18-258.

4. Readers may recall my discussion at the end of chapter 5 about Batya, the blind girl whose Orthodox Jewish community rallied to support her reading from the Torah during her bat mitzvah. As I note several times throughout the book, one of the challenges for blind Jews is that there are competing interpretations about whether or not a blind

Jew, especially a blind rabbi, is allowed to find alternative methods for "reading" the Torah. Some rabbinical teachings decree that one must use one's eyes to legitimately read, while other rabbinical teachings adhere to a broader definition of "reading." Orthodox Jews tend to be more literal in their interpretations of biblical instructions, especially as they pertain to issues such as gender and disability, which is why it is particularly noteworthy that Batya's community supported her Torah reading.

5. Brian Watermeyer and Leslie Swartz, "Disablism, Identity and Self: Discrimination as a Traumatic Assault on Subjectivity," *Journal of Community & Applied Social Psychology* 26, no. 3 (2016), https://doi.org/10 .1002/casp.2266.

6. Watermeyer and Swartz, "Disablism, Identity and Self."

7. Johanna Hedva, "Sick Woman Theory," accessed July 17, 2024, https:// www.kunstverein-hildesheim.de/assets/bilder/caring-structures -ausstellung-digital/Johanna-Hedva/cb6ec5c75f/AUSSTELLUNG_1110 _Hedva_SWT_e.pdf.

8. Piepzna-Samarasinha, *Care Work*.

9. bell hooks, *Killing Rage: Ending Racism* (New York: Henry Holt, 1995), 265.

10. Keri Day, *Religious Resistance to Neoliberalism: Womanist and Feminist Perspectives* (London: Palgrave Macmillan, 2015), 105.

11. Day, *Religious Resistance to Neoliberalism*, 106.

12. Day, *Religious Resistance to Neoliberalism*, 106.

13. Day, *Religious Resistance to Neoliberalism*, 117.

14. Slavoj Zizek, quoted in Day, *Religious Resistance to Neoliberalism*, 117.

15. Day, *Religious Resistance to Neoliberalism*, 117.

16. Lauren Tuchman, "ELI Talk: We All Were at Sinai: The Transformative Power of Inclusive Torah," last modified December 11, 2017, https://rabbituchman.com/2017/12/11/eli-talk-we-all-were-at-sinai-the -transformative-power-of-inclusive-torah/.

17. One of the earliest references to this phrase comes from James Charlton, who used it as the title for his book, *Nothing About Us Without Us: Disability Oppression and Empowerment* (Berkeley: University of California Press, 1998), after hearing it used by South African disability activists. David Werner published a book that same year and also used the phrase

in his title: *Nothing About Us Without Us: Developing Innovative Technologies for, by, and with Disabled Persons* (Lakeport, Calif.: HealthWrights, 1998). Since the publication of these books, the phrase has become common usage in the United States in the disability rights movement, in disability communities generally, and among disability activists.

Bibliography

Boornstein, Michelle. "A Bat Mitzvah Girl Debuts a New Way for Blind Jews to Participate in an Ancient Tradition." *Washington Post*, January 14, 2019. https://www.washingtonpost.com/religion/2019/01/14/bat-mitzvah -girl-debuts-new-way-blind-jews-participate-an-ancient-tradition/.

Bracey, Glenn, and Wendy Moore. "'Race Tests': Racial Boundary Maintenance in White Evangelical Churches." *Sociological Inquiry* 87, no. 2 (May 2017): 282–302.

Calder, Andy. "'God Has Chosen This for You'—'Really?' A Pastoral and Theological Appraisal of This and Some Other Well-Known Clichés Used in Australia to Support People with Disabilities." *Journal for Religion, Health and Disability* 8, no. 1/2 (2004): 5–19.

Centers for Disease Control and Prevention. "Adults with Disabilities: Ethnicity and Race Infographic." Accessed January 6, 2023. https://www.cdc .gov/disability-and-health/articles-documents/infographic-adults-with -disabilities-ethnicity-and-race.html?CDC_AAref_Val=https://www .cdc.gov/ncbddd/disabilityandhealth/materials/infographic-disabilities -ethnicity-race.html.

Centers for Disease Control and Prevention. "Disability Impacts All of Us Infographic." Last modified May 15, 2023. https://www.cdc.gov/ disability-and-health/articles-documents/disability-impacts-all-of-us -infographic.html?CDC_AAref_Val=https://www.cdc.gov/ncbddd/ disabilityandhealth/infographic-disability-impacts-all.html.

Charlton, James. *Nothing About Us Without Us: Disability Oppression and Empowerment*. Berkeley: University of California Press, 1998.

Clare, Eli. *Exile and Pride: Disability, Queerness, and Liberation*. Durham, N.C.: Duke University Press, 2015.

Columbia Law School. "Kimberlé Crenshaw on Intersectionality, More Than Two Decades Later." Last modified June 8, 2017. https://www.law .columbia.edu/news/archive/kimberle-crenshaw-intersectionality-more -two-decades-later.

Davis, Lennard J., ed. *The Disability Studies Reader.* 5th ed. New York: Routledge, 2017.

Day, Keri. *Religious Resistance to Neoliberalism: Womanist and Feminist Perspectives.* London: Palgrave Macmillan, 2015.

Eiesland, Nancy. *The Disabled God: Toward a Liberatory Theology of Disability.* Nashville, Tenn.: Abingdon Press, 1994.

Foucault, Michel. "The Subject and Power." *Critical Inquiry* 8, no. 4 (1982): 777–795. Accessed July 5, 2024. https://doi.org/10.1086/448181.

Garland-Thomson, Rosemarie. "Feminist Disability Studies." *Signs: Journal of Women in Culture and Society* 30, no. 2 (2005): 1557–1587. https://doi .org/10.1086/423352.

Garland-Thomson, Rosemarie. "Misfits: A Feminist Materialist Disability Concept." *Hypatia* 26, no. 3, (2011): 591–609. *JSTOR,* https://www.jstor .org/stable/23016570.

Garland-Thomson, Rosemarie. "Staring at the Other." *Disability Studies Quarterly* 25, no. 4 (2005). https://doi.org/10.18061/dsq.v25i4.

Goggin, Gerard, and Christopher Newell. "Fame and Disability: Christopher Reeve, Super Crips, and Infamous Celebrity." *M/C Journal* 7, no. 5 (2004). https://doi.org/10.5204/mcj.2404.

Government Accountability Office. "K-12 Education: Discipline Disparities for Black Students, Boys, and Students with Disabilities." Last modified March 22, 2018. https://www.gao.gov/products/gao-18-258.

Harrison, Beverly Wildung, and Carol S. Robb. *Making the Connections: Essays in Feminist Social Ethics.* Boston: Beacon Press, 1986.

Hedva, Johanna. "Sick Woman Theory." Accessed July 17, 2024. https://www .kunstverein-hildesheim.de/assets/bilder/caring-structures-ausstellung -digital/Johanna-Hedva/cb6ec5c75f/AUSSTELLUNG_1110_Hedva _SWT_e.pdf.

Heumann, Judith, and John Wodatch. "We're 20 Percent of America, and We're Still Invisible." *New York Times,* July 26, 2020. https://www .nytimes.com/2020/07/26/opinion/Americans-with-disabilities-act .html.

Hill Collins, Patricia. *Black Feminist Thought: Knowledge, Consciousness, and the Politics of Empowerment.* 10th ed. New York: Routledge, 2000.

hooks, bell. *Killing Rage: Ending Racism.* New York: Henry Holt, 1995.

James, Christine. "Catholicism and Disability: Sacred and Profane." In *Judaism, Christianity, and Islam: Sacred Texts, Historical Traditions, and Social Analysis,* edited by Darla Schumm and Michael Stoltzfus, 167–185. New York: Palgrave Macmillan, 2011.

Kafai, Shayda. "Crafting Disabled Sexuality: The Visual Language of Nomy Lamm's 'Wall of Fire.'" In *Bodies in Commotion: Disability & Performance,* edited by Carrie Sandahl and Philip Auslander, 179–191. Ann Arbor: University of Michigan Press, 2005.

Kafer, Alison. "Compulsory Bodies: Reflections on Heterosexuality and Able-Bodiedness." *Journal of Women's History* 15, no. 3 (2003): 77–89.

Kafer, Alison. *Feminist, Queer, Crip.* Bloomington: Indiana University Press, 2013.

Koosed, Jennifer, and Darla Schumm. "Out of the Darkness: Examining the Rhetoric of Blindness in the Gospel of John." *Disability Studies Quarterly* 25, no. 1 (2005). https://doi.org/10.18061/dsq.v25i1.528.

Luther, Martin. "Let Your Sins Be Strong: A Letter from Luther to Melanchthon." Project Wittenberg. Accessed July 23, 2024. https://www.projectwittenberg.org/pub/resources/text/wittenberg/luther/letsinsbe.txt.

McRuer, Robert. *Crip Theory: Cultural Signs of Queerness and Disability.* New York: New York University Press, 2006.

Millett-Gallant, Ann, and Elizabeth Howie, eds. *Disability and Art History.* 1st ed. London: Routledge, 2016.

Nixon, Rob. *Slow Violence and the Environmentalism of the Poor.* Cambridge, Mass.: Harvard University Press, 2011.

Oliver, Michael. *The Politics of Disablement: A Sociological Approach.* New York: St. Martin's Press, 1990.

Owens, Lama Rod. *Love and Rage: The Path of Liberation Through Anger.* Berkeley: North Atlantic Books, 2020.

Pheterson, Gail. "Alliances Between Women: Overcoming Internalized Oppression and Internalized Domination." *Signs: Journal of Women in Culture and Society* 12, no. 1 (1986): 146–160. https://doi-org.hollins.idm.oclc.org/10.1086/494302.

Piepzna-Samarasinha, Leah Lakshmi. *Care Work: Dreaming Disability Justice.* Vancouver: Arsenal Pulp, 2018.

Public Religion Research Institute (PRRI). "The 2020 Census of American Religion." PRRI. Last modified July 8, 2021. https://www.prri.org/research/2020-census-of-american-religion/.

Said, Edward. *Orientalism.* New York: Penguin Random House, 1979.

Samuels, Ellen. "Slow Time, Slow Futurity." *Panorama: Journal of the Association of Historians of American Art* 8, no. 1 (Spring 2022). https://doi.org/10.24926/24716839.13275.

Sandahl, Carrie. "Queering the Crip or Cripping the Queer? Intersections of Queer and Crip Identities in Solo Autobiographical Performance." *GLQ* 9, nos. 1–2 (April 2003): 25–56. https://doi.org/10.1215/10642684-9-1-2-25.

Schriempf, Alexa. "(Re)fusing the Amputated Body: An Interactionist Bridge for Feminism and Disability." *Hypatia* 16, no. 4 (2001): 56–72. *JSTOR*, https://www.jstor.org/stable/3810783.

Schumm, Darla. "It's Time for 'Crip Time.'" *Inside Higher Ed,* June 26, 2022. https://www.insidehighered.com/views/2022/06/27/adopt-crip-time-make-higher-ed-more-inclusive-opinion.

Serendip Studio. "Supercrip and the Politics of Pity." Last modified September 8, 2014. https://serendipstudio.org/oneworld/identity-matters-being-belonging-becoming/supercrip-and-politics-pity.

Shakespeare, Tom. *Disability Rights and Wrongs Revisited.* 2nd ed. New York: Routledge, 2014.

Siebers, Tobin. *Disability Aesthetics.* Ann Arbor: University of Michigan Press, 2010.

Smith, Jean Edward. *FDR.* New York: Random House, 2008.

Spurrier, Rebecca F. *The Disabled Church: Human Difference and the Art of Communal Worship.* New York: Fordham University Press, 2019.

Strauss, Valerie. "Implicit Racial Bias Causes Black Boys to Be Disciplined at School More Than Whites, Federal Report Finds." *Washington Post,* April 5, 2018. https://www.washingtonpost.com/news/answer-sheet/wp/2018/04/05/implicit-racial-bias-causes-black-boys-to-be-disciplined-at-school-more-than-whites-federal-report-finds/.

Tuchman, Lauren. "ELI Talk: We All Were at Sinai: The Transformative Power of Inclusive Torah." Last modified December 11, 2017. https://

rabbituchman.com/2017/12/11/eli-talk-we-all-were-at-sinai-the
-transformative-power-of-inclusive-torah/.

UD Project. "What Is Universal Design?" Accessed June 6, 2024. https://
universaldesign.org/definition.

United Nations. "Factsheet on Persons with Disabilities." Accessed February 6, 2023. https://www.un.org/development/desa/disabilities/resources/
factsheet-on-persons-with-disabilities.html.

U.S. Department of Justice. "Guide to Disability Rights Laws." Last modified February 28, 2020. https://www.ada.gov/resources/disability-rights
-guide/.

Vacek, Heather. *Madness: American Protestant Responses to Mental Illness.*
Waco, Tex.: Baylor University Press, 2015.

Watermeyer, Brian, and Leslie Swartz. "Disablism, Identity and Self: Discrimination as a Traumatic Assault on Subjectivity." *Journal of Community & Applied Social Psychology* 26, no. 3 (2016). https://doi.org/10.1002/
casp.2266.

Watts Belser, Julia. *Loving Our Own Bones: Disability Wisdom and the Spiritual Subversiveness of Knowing Ourselves Whole.* Boston: Beacon Press,
2023.

Werner, David. *Nothing About Us Without Us: Developing Innovative Technologies for, by, and with Disabled Persons.* Lakeport, Calif.: HealthWrights,
1998.

Young, Stella. "Inspiration Porn and the Objectification of Disability:
Stella Young." TEDxSydney. https://youtu.be/SxrS7-I_sMQ?si=
3uaPgS2KuwC2-4.

Young, Stella. "We're Not Here for Your Inspiration." Ramp Up. Last modified July 2, 2012. https://www.abc.net.au/rampup/articles/2012/07/02/
3537035.htm.

About the Author

DARLA SCHUMM is a disabled author and educator. She is the associate provost for curriculum and faculty engagement at Hollins University. Schumm has authored numerous articles and coedited four books exploring intersections of disability and the world's religions, most recently *Disability and World Religions: An Introduction*. Schumm lives in the Blue Ridge Mountains with her husband, son, and two dogs. She is an avid knitter and powerlifter.